A HEALTHY KIDS' COOKBOOK

Kid Smoothies

Kid Smoothies

A HEALTHY KIDS' COOKBOOK

Smoothie Recipes Kids Will love to Make

ERIN FLETTER

Food Geek in Chief and Co-Founder
of Sticky Fingers Cooking

Photography by Clare Barboza

Z Kids • New York

To every one of our kid chefs around the world: Your excitement for cooking and trying new things inspires us every day!

Contents

SMOOTHIES

SMOOTHIE BOWLS

SMOOTHIE POPS

Introduction

Hi there!

Welcome to your very own smoothie cookbook! Icy, creamy, mouthwatering treats you can make in your own kitchen—what could be better?

In this book, you'll find step-by-step instructions and pictures designed to teach you how to make tasty, slurpable, healthy delights at home. Learn to make sippable smoothies, smoothie bowls with tasty mix-ins and toppings, and refreshing smoothie pops—before you know it, you'll become a smoothie master!

I'm so excited to share this book with you, because smoothies are:

- Fun, fast, and easy to make

- Healthy and give us energy

- Impressive to friends and family

- Something I've loved forever!

When I was a kid, my mom would make delicious smoothies for me every day before school. I remember learning how to make them with her. I remember the excitement I felt when she let me choose which fresh, colorful fruits to add to the blender. I loved the loud whirring sound of the blender because I knew that delicious smoothie was coming soon!

We practiced peeling, cutting, and blending, and before long, I was making yummy smoothies for her! Years later, I taught my own kids how to make them. We loved our smoothies so much, I even started Sticky Fingers Cooking, a cooking school where we have taught *thousands* of kids how to make smoothies and lots more!

Now that you're learning the smoothie ropes, I hope this book will help you feel at home in your kitchen. The more you make, the more you'll learn, and soon you'll be confidently cutting, bravely blending, and then actually *inventing* your own recipes, mixing and matching different flavors to see what *you* like best! It's the greatest feeling ever. Just wait and see.

So, let's get started, but first . . . (everything's better with a joke).

What's a cow's favorite drink? *A s-moooo-thie, of course!*

Cheers!

Erin Fletter
Food Geek in Chief of Sticky Fingers Cooking

Before You Get Started

It's important to keep safety in mind as you handle and prepare ingredients and kitchen tools and equipment. Please read these essential kitchen safety rules. These guidelines will help you be safe in the kitchen as you build your smoothie skills.

Safety First

Dress the part. Have you ever noticed how chefs dress? They dress safely to protect themselves from kitchen hazards. Roll up your sleeves, and remove any rings or dangling bracelets so they don't get in your way.

Hair's the thing! Nobody wants to find hair in their smoothie! If you have long hair, tie it back or tuck it under a hat like the pros.

Handle sharp objects with care. Practice cutting, grating, and blending fruits and vegetables with an adult before trying to do it on your own.

Clean up quick to avoid a slip. If an ingredient spills or lands on the floor, clean it up right away to avoid slips or falls. It's also a good idea to wear shoes or socks to prevent slipping.

Ask for help. Don't be afraid to ask an adult for help if you need it or have questions. Asking questions is a big part of learning—even the best chefs are always learning!

Kitchen Basics

Keep germs away. To avoid spreading germs, always wash your hands with soap and water before handling food. Also, make sure all your equipment (blenders, utensils, measuring cups, etc.) is clean before you use it.

Know where you're headed. Always start by reading the recipe from beginning to end. This will help you understand each recipe and feel comfortable as you tackle it, plus you'll know what you need.

Hunt and gather. Gather all equipment and ingredients before you start. Blender? Check! Frozen fruit? Check! Milk? Check!

Take your time. Take it slow, and follow the recipe directions carefully. This way, you'll be sure to use the correct ingredient in the right amount.

Beware of blades. Be safe around sharp knives and blades, even when you're not using them. Ask an adult for help cutting or chopping, if needed. Always wash and put away a knife after you're finished using it.

Clean as you go. This will save you a big mess at the end. Clean up any spills or messes as soon as they happen; put utensils, cups, and bowls in the dishwasher or wash them right away; put away ingredients after adding them; and wash the blender as soon as you're done with it.

Blender Basics

Using a blender can be fun, but it's important to use it safely. With a little practice and skill, you'll be whipping up delicious smoothies, smoothie bowls, and smoothie pops in no time!

There are different kinds of blenders:

Countertop This blender has a removable pitcher or jar that attaches to a mechanical base.

Handheld This is a long, stick-shaped tool with a blade at one end. This can be placed directly into a bowl or a pot filled with ingredients for blending. It's also known as an immersion blender.

Personal This blender has personal or individual-size containers that attach to a mechanical base and double as to-go cups.

We used a countertop blender for the recipes in this book, but you can use whatever you have at home. A handheld blender will help chop the fruits and vegetables into smaller pieces. If using this type of blender, use crushed ice instead of cubes. If you use a personal blender, cut the recipe ingredients in half because they won't all fit.

Blending Safety Tips

Put a lid on it. Always make sure the lid is securely fitted onto the blender before turning it on.

Start slow to go fast. Start blending your smoothie ingredients on a low speed first, and work your way up to a higher speed to ensure a safe and smooth blend. Some blenders might only have one speed, and that's okay. You can still start slowly by pulsing the blender. *Pulse, pulse, blend!*

Play keep-away. When the blender motor is on, clear the space around it, including your hands. Don't place anything into a blender when it's running, including spatulas, ingredients, utensils, and especially hands. *Always turn the blender off and unplug it before taking the lid off.*

Keep the base dry. Water and electricity don't mix well, so keep the blender base and power cord dry at all times. Never put the base of the blender in water. When cleaning the blender, always detach the pitcher from the base to wash the pitcher. You can wipe the base with a damp cloth if food gets on it.

Don't force it. If the blender is not blending, turn it off, unplug it, and ask an adult to help you figure out what's wrong.

Blend Like a Pro!

- If you have too much frozen fruits/vegetables or ice, the blender will get stuck and won't blend properly. Don't worry, just add more liquid, like milk, juice, or water.

- Let frozen fruits and veggies thaw for a few minutes before blending.

- Before blending, always start with liquids, then add soft ingredients like nut or seed butters, tofu, or fresh produce, and add the frozen stuff last!

Microplane

Juicer

Colander

Measuring cups

Measuring
spoons

Paring knife

Cutting board

Peeler

Prep Like a Pro

Washing and preparing fruits and veggies is important for smoothie making. It's also a basic skill that's handy for making other things, like school lunches and meals. Keep learning and practicing basic cooking skills, and soon you'll be ready for even more kitchen adventures!

Washing Your Vegetables and Fruits

Removing dirt and germs that fruits and veggies may have picked up on the way to your kitchen will make your smoothies safe to eat. Here's how to do it:

Clean + rub. Before cutting into it, give the whole fruit or vegetable a gentle rub under a stream of cold water to remove any dirt or germs. Try to catch every corner and cranny!

Scrub bumpy skins. Some fruit and veggies will still have dirt on them from the soil they grow in! This is especially true for produce with bumpy skin, like melons and carrots. Hold the fruit or veggie under cold water and rub away any dirt and germs, or use a vegetable brush to scrub gently.

Rinse before peeling. Rinse all produce before peeling it, even if you don't plan to eat the peel. This helps prevent the spread of dirt and germs.

Keep it clean. Use a clean kitchen towel for drying fruits and vegetables after washing. A dirty towel can spread germs.

When in doubt, cut it out. Cut away any damaged or bruised areas before preparing or eating.

HELPFUL KITCHEN TOOLS FOR WASHING

Salad spinner (or colander): A salad spinner can dry washed leafy greens, like spinach and kale. If you don't have a salad spinner, a colander will do the trick!

Kitchen towels: You can use either paper or cloth towels to dry your produce.

Vegetable brush: Use this for scrubbing fruits and vegetables that have bumpy skins, like carrots and cucumbers.

Measuring spoons

Measuring cups

Contain the mess!

Measuring

When you're new to making smoothies, measuring tools can help you determine the proper amounts of each ingredient so your smoothie turns out great every time! Here's what you'll need:

Measuring cups Use for large amounts of liquid, like yogurt, milk, or juice.

Measuring spoons These are great for small amounts of wet and dry ingredients, like honey, vanilla extract, or spices.

Your hands That's a tool for measuring every pinch, drizzle, sprinkle, and squeeze!

PRO TIPS FOR MEASURING

Level up. Place the measuring cup on a flat surface before pouring in your liquid to help get an accurate measurement.

Prevent sticky situations. If you have cooking spray available, spray the inside of your measuring spoon or cup when measuring sticky liquids like honey or peanut butter to keep the liquid from sticking and make cleanup easier.

Contain the mess. Using a measuring spoon can be messy sometimes. A good trick is to hold the spoon over an empty bowl while you measure. This way, if anything spills while you're measuring, it will fall into the bowl instead of on the counter. So much easier to clean up!

Turn clumps into cups. It's hard to measure frozen fruits and veggies when the pieces are frozen into big clumps. Let the produce thaw for a few minutes, then use a spoon or fork to break it into smaller pieces that you can measure.

Eyeball it. It's hard to mess up a smoothie. If your measurements aren't exact, that's okay. You may even decide to change the measurements on purpose once you've tried the smoothie. There's nothing wrong with adding a little more banana or berries if you like the flavor!

Peeling

Making smoothies sometimes involves peeling fruits and veggies. It's easy when you have the right tools and tips. Here's what you'll need:

Bowl Keep your ingredients in a bowl until you're ready to use them. A bowl is also good for catching peelings and scraps and keeping them all in one place.

Cutting board Important to use to protect your countertop or table.

Paring knife This is a small knife used for cutting fruits and veggies and removing stems and seeds.

Peeler This removes skins from certain fruits and veggies. There are different types of peelers—some are straight, and others are Y-shaped. Both work well!

Spoon Use one for removing fresh ginger skin (see Pro Tip following).

PRO TIPS FOR PEELING

Peel like a pro—safely! Hold the peeler with your dominant hand (are you a righty or a lefty?) and the vegetable with the other. Securely hold the vegetable with your hand, or place it on the cutting board for more support. Protect your fingers—tuck them away from the blade. Next, press the blade of the peeler firmly against the vegetable's skin and push it away from your body. The trick is in the amount of pressure you use: not too much, and not too little! Go slowly with each swipe.

Peel it and clear it. Once you finish peeling, clear away all the peels and skins from the cutting board so they're not in your way.

Do you know that you can use a spoon to peel fresh ginger? First, hold the spoon in your dominant hand and the root in your other hand. Press the edge of the spoon firmly against the ginger, then push the spoon away from you and— *ta-da!*—the skin will flake right off.

For an easy way to peel an orange, start by cutting it in half so the stem part is at one end. Next, turn the halves inside out, then pop out the pieces inside. The halved segments will easily pull away from the skin.

Cutting

This section teaches you about the tools you'll use for cutting produce. We know that handling kitchen blades can be scary at first, so here are some tips to help you feel more confident and safe as you build your knife skills.

Cutting board Use a cutting board to protect the countertop or table. Make sure the cutting board is secure and sits flat on the countertop before using it.

Safety knife A plastic knife with "teeth" is a safe tool to use when you're new to knives. When you and your caregiver feel ready, you can start using a sharp metal knife.

Sharp paring knife Make sure your knife is sharp! It's easier to control the blade of a sharp knife, so you're less likely to hurt yourself. Dull blades can be dangerous, so stay sharp and stay safe!

PRO TIPS FOR CUTTING

Keep it steady and clear. When cutting fruits and veggies, it's important to work on a flat surface like a cutting board. Make sure to clear the space around your workstation.

Flat is where it's at. Always lay food down flat before cutting it. If the food is round (like carrots and apples), ask an adult to cut a flat edge on it so it won't roll. This makes it safer and easier to practice your skills.

Hold on. With your dominant hand, grip the knife at the top of the handle where the blade and handle meet. This makes it easier to control the knife.

MAKE A BEAR CLAW Curl all the fingers and the thumb of your other hand like you're imitating a bear clawing. Then, place the claw on the food you want to cut, pressing the tips of your fingernails against the food to hold it in place. Then, take your knife and slowly saw into the produce with a back-and-forth motion until the blade cuts through the produce and touches the cutting board. This helps keep your fingers safe while you cut. Try keeping your elbows close to your body for a steadier cut.

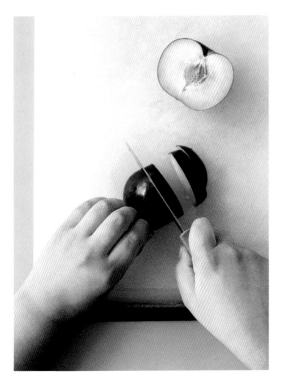

Ask for help! Everyone needs help sometimes (even grown-ups), and getting help from an adult can make things easier and safer while you get the hang of your new skills.

Why should you never argue with a knife? Because it will always have a good point!

How to Prep an Avocado

What You'll Need
- Ripe avocado (unripe avocados don't taste very good, and they're difficult to work with)
- Clean, dry kitchen towel
- Cutting board
- Sharp paring knife or safety knife
- Spoon
- Bowl

1. Use a paring knife to carefully cut all the way around a clean and dry avocado lengthwise.

2. Gently twist both halves of the avocado . . .

3. . . . and pull the halves apart.

4. Use your thumb to pop out the pit by pushing behind it.

5. Scrape the avocado fruit into a bowl.

How to Grate a Carrot

What You'll Need
- Carrot
- Vegetable brush (optional)
- Clean, dry kitchen towel
- Cutting board
- Sharp paring knife
- Grater

1. Rinse the carrot under cold running water and use a vegetable brush to scrub away any visible dirt.

2. Pat the carrot dry with a clean towel.

3. Use a paring knife to carefully cut off both ends of the carrot.

4. Place the grater on top of a cutting board to catch the grated carrot. Make sure the cutting board is on a flat and stable surface.

5. Place one hand on the grater to keep it steady. With your other hand, press the carrot against the side of the grater and push down firmly. Finish grating when your fingers get close to the grater—don't grate your fingers!

How to Zest Citrus

What You'll Need

- Any citrus fruit
- Clean, dry kitchen towel
- Small bowl
- Zesting tool (like a Microplane, zester, or grater with fine holes)

1. Rinse the fruit under cold running water. and pat the fruit dry with a clean towel.

2. Place a bowl on the counter or table in front of you. (You could also zest directly into a blender pitcher or smoothie instead.)

3. Hold the fruit in your dominant hand and the zesting tool in the other.

4. Slowly and carefully press the fruit against the sharp side of the zesting tool and push down firmly. Be sure to keep your fingers from touching the zesting tool—it's very sharp!

5. Be sure to zest only the colored skin of the fruit and not the bitter white part.

Freezing + Storing

Some recipes use fruits and veggies that are already frozen. If you have some leftover fresh produce, freezing it is a good way to save the produce and keep it fresh. This section teaches you how to freeze and store ingredients so they stay tasty and are ready to use the next time you make a smoothie. Here are some materials that can help you freeze and store like a pro!

Rimmed baking sheet Use this for freezing berries and fruit.

Freezer storage bags These are airtight and will keep food fresh longer.

Permanent marker Use a dark color for labeling freezer bag contents.

Ice cube trays These are great for freezing leftover smoothie in smaller portions.

PRO TIPS FOR FREEZING + STORING

Chill out. Freeze any sliced ripe avocado meat or bananas for future smoothie making—just remember to peel them first.

Try the "berry best" freezing method. Wash and dry the berries, then remove any stems. Next, spread the berries evenly on a rimmed baking sheet so no berries are touching. This allows the berries to freeze individually, instead of in clumps that are difficult to work with. Try this for cut fruit, too!

Bag and tag. Before freezing foods, label the container or bag with its contents and the date to keep track of what's in the bag and how long it has been in the freezer. It's much easier to write on a freezer bag *before* filling it!

Freeze with ease. Pour leftover smoothies into ice cube trays, pop them into the freezer, and they'll be ready next time you want to make a smoothie.

Keep it creamy. For smoothie bowls that are as thick and creamy as ice cream, start with frozen fruit. Don't add water or ice—they'll make the smoothie bowl less creamy.

3 Tips for the Creamiest Blends

For the creamiest smoothies, try using one or more of these frozen fruits or veggies:

- Avocado
- Banana
- Coconut
- Mango
- Peaches
- Zucchini

Nut butters, seed butters, and beans also add creaminess. Try:

- Almond butter
- Cashew butter
- Cooked white beans (also called cannellini, navy, or Great Northern beans)
- Peanut butter
- Sunflower seed butter
- Tahini paste
- Tofu (silken)

Dairy and alternative milks and cheeses are another add-in for a creamy texture. Consider:

- Coconut cream
- Coconut milk (full-fat)
- Cottage cheese
- Cream cheese
- Dairy-free yogurt (as long as it's thick and creamy, like Greek yogurt)
- Greek yogurt
- Ricotta cheese
- Sour cream

Build Your Smoothie

Are you ready to learn how to make mouthwatering smoothies? In this section, you'll learn how to choose the best fruits and veggies, mix delicious flavor combinations, and add over-the-top toppings.

Eat All the Colors and More

Most fruits and veggies are called "superfoods" because they're loaded with vitamins and minerals that help keep your body and brain healthy and fit. Smoothies are an easy—and delicious!—way to get the nutrition you need. The more colorful your fruits and veggies are, the more nutrients you'll get from them. Let's try to "eat the rainbow" every day! Here are the top ten fruits and veggies in this book that pack a nutritional punch:

Avocados are full of healthy fats called omega-3 fatty acids. Omega-3 fatty acids help your brain and heart work better. To select a good avocado, look for one with dark green–black skin. When you press a ripe avocado, it will be firm but bounce back with a little squeeze. Try popping off the stem and looking at the spot inside the fruit. If the spot is green, the avocado is good. If it's brown or black, move on—it's overripe.

Bananas contain potassium, which helps your heart stay healthy so it can pump blood throughout your body. When choosing bananas at the grocery store, look for firm bananas that are yellow (not green) without too many brown spots.

Beets contain antioxidants that help our red blood cells stay healthy. When choosing beets at the market, find medium-size beets with smooth, dark skin and no cracks or soft spots. You can also use canned beets (not pickled).

Carrots are loaded with vitamin A, which is great for your eyesight; it also helps you grow strong bones and teeth! Look for crisp, bright-colored carrots—not soft or bendy ones.

Dates are sometimes called "nature's candy" because they taste like caramel! Dates have tons of fiber, which helps you digest food and keeps you feeling full. Dried dates are usually sold in the produce section near the fruits and veggies. If your store has fresh dates, look for those that are shiny and chubby, and avoid dry, hard ones because they may not be as fresh. Also, some dates have pits that should be removed.

Green peas have protein to help muscles grow. Both frozen and fresh work well! Frozen peas can be found in the frozen aisle at the market, and if you're choosing fresh, look for crisp, plump pods or plump, round peas!

Limes are a great source of vitamin C, which helps your body stay healthy and strong. To choose a good lime, look for one that feels heavy for its size. The skin should be bright green and have no spots. When you press the lime with the pad of a finger, the skin should bounce back quickly—that tells you it's ripe.

Pineapples have an enzyme called bromelain that helps your body break down and digest food. Enzymes speed up chemical reactions in our bodies, which is why eating lots of fresh pineapple makes your tongue feel fuzzy! When choosing a pineapple, look for one with golden-yellow skin that's firm but not hard as a rock. It should feel heavy and smell sweet and fruity.

Spinach contains iron, which gives us energy and keeps our body strong. When choosing spinach, look for crisp, bright-green leaves. Skip any bunches with wilted or dark, slimy leaves.

Zucchini contains potassium, which keeps your heart pumping strong! When choosing a zucchini, look for one with smooth, shiny skin.

Yummy Mix-Ins: Chef Challenge—Be Bold and Adventurous!

This section encourages you to explore some fun and tasty toppings that you can layer in to add flavors and textures to your smoothies and smoothie bowls. When you get to the recipes, you might see some familiar ingredients, and maybe meet some new ones that are less common but easily found at a local grocery store. Try taking your taste buds for an adventure with some of these new flavors! Do they tingle and dance when you try something new? If you're not ready, that's okay, too! We'll provide alternative options with easily recognized ingredients.

Cocoa powder contains antioxidants, which are like tiny superheroes that protect the cells in your body from damage. Cocoa powder is a healthy source of smooth chocolatey flavor without the sugar!

Coconut is an excellent source of fiber and fat. Fiber helps you digest food, and fat gives you energy. Adding different types of coconut can change how the smoothie or smoothie bowl feels in your mouth. Experiment: Compare the crunch of shredded and flaked coconut, or try the creaminess of sweetened and toasted coconut.

Dairy and dairy-free substitutes, including cow's milk and plant-based milk and yogurts, offer a wide variety of nutrients and add creaminess to smoothies. Some recipes in this book specify the type of milk or yogurt that works best in those recipes, such as "whole milk" or "Greek yogurt." Other recipes will say "milk of choice" or simply "yogurt." Use what you like and experiment! It's just important to know that some milks (like almond and coconut milk) will add a different flavor, and some milks (like coconut milk) will create a creamier texture. The same goes for different types of yogurt.

Fresh mint freshens your breath and helps the body fight infection. Plop a few fragrant leaves on your smoothie for a fresh, bright minty flavor and a pop of color!

Nut butter is a good source of fiber, fat, and protein—these keep our bodies fueled with energy. Protein also helps your muscles and bones grow. Peanut butter is the popular choice, but any nut butter can be a healthy way to naturally add creaminess and nutty flavors to your recipes!

Oats are a good source of zinc, which helps heal cuts and scrapes. Quick oats and rolled oats add chewiness to a smoothie. If you love a good crunch, try a handful of granola—that's made from oats!

Seeds such as sunflower, pumpkin, sesame, and chia, contain vitamin E. This vitamin protects your eyes and keeps your skin healthy. Sprinkle them on a smoothie or smoothie bowl for a crispy crunch!

Tofu is made from soybeans. It's a great source of protein that helps your body grow strong muscles and gives you the energy to do the things you love. All types of tofu (firm, soft, silken) can give your smoothies a boost of creaminess. You can usually find tofu in a refrigerated section of the grocery store.

YOU—don't forget the most important ingredient: your curiosity, your taste for adventure, and your readiness to try new flavors and textures!

Allergies: Food for Thought

Some people have food allergies, which are special challenges with eating certain foods. Food allergies can be mild or very serious, so it's important to be careful when cooking and eating.

Some common allergens in smoothies or smoothie pops include milk, peanuts, sesame, soybeans (like tofu), tree nuts, and wheat, and some lesser-known but still common allergens include avocados and bananas. But don't worry; there are always substitutions you can make for any ingredient so everyone can enjoy your yummy treats. Here are some of our favorite swaps for common allergens in smoothies and smoothie pops:

AVOCADO: Silken tofu, Greek yogurt, and coconut cream provide a similar creaminess.

BANANAS: Mango or papaya provides a similar sweetness and creaminess.

MILK: Any plant-based milk, like almond, soy, or oat milk, will work well.

PEANUTS: Other nut butters, like almond or cashew butter, are good replacements. For a nut-free option, try seed butter, like sunflower, pumpkin, or sesame (tahini).

SESAME SEEDS: Other seeds are good substitutes. Try chia, flax, or hemp seeds. For a nutty flavor, you can also use almond or peanut butter.

TOFU: Any plant-based protein, like pea, hemp, or rice protein powder, will work. For non-plant-based options, Greek yogurt is a great substitution for silken tofu.

TREE NUTS: Other nuts, like almonds, cashews, or walnuts, are great replacements. For a nut-free option, try sunflower, pumpkin, or sesame seeds.

WHEAT: Gluten-free oats, quinoa flakes, or rice flakes work well. You could also use almond flour or coconut flour.

Mixing and Matching

How do you know which flavor combinations will make a smoothie taste good? In this section, you'll learn about popular flavor combinations. Before long, you'll be mixing and matching ingredients to create your very own smoothie recipes!

Beets + Berries It's no wonder this is such a popular smoothie pairing— beets and berries complement each other with flavor and nutrition! The sweetness of the beets balances the tartness of the berries. Beets and berries are loaded with antioxidants, the superheroes in your bodies that fight cell damage. Try the Heart Beet Smoothie on page 70.

Lemon + Blueberry Can you guess why these flavors go great together? It's because the blueberry's sweetness mellows out the lemon's tartness. Also, blueberries and lemons both have vitamin C, working as a team to help your body fight off germs! Try the Very Berry Zest Quest on page 69.

Lime + Coconut Why are lime and coconut such a dynamite duo? Well, you might taste hints of vanilla and almond in the coconut and the lime's zingy freshness to create a burst of flavors on your taste buds! Plus, when eaten together, the fat from the coconut helps your body absorb the vitamin C from the lime. That's some real teamwork! Try the Totally Tropicool Fruit Smoothie on page 87.

Pineapple + Orange + Ginger This tried-and-true flavor trio works because the sweetness from the pineapple and orange works well with the ginger's zestiness. All three ingredients contain vitamin C, so this smoothie combo is more than refreshing; it's a blast of super-nutrients! Try the Pineapple Paradise on page 84.

Spinach + Apple + Banana These ingredients are a winning combination because the sweetness of the apple and banana balances the mild bitterness of the spinach. There is also some nutritional magic at work: Apples and bananas contain vitamin C, and spinach contains iron. Your body absorbs iron better when you eat it with vitamin C! Try the Tres Amigas Avocado Batido on page 63.

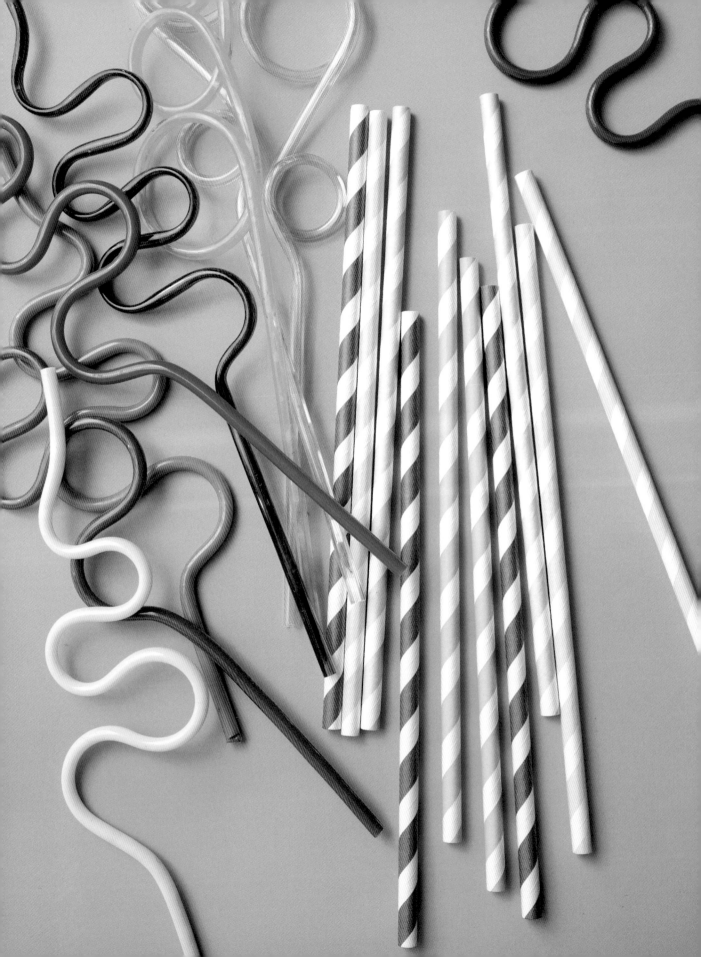

The Recipes

· · · · · · · · · · · · · ·

Before we start, here's what the labels on the recipes mean:

5 INGREDIENT

This means the recipe has 5 or fewer ingredients, not including ice or water.

DAIRY-FREE, GLUTEN-FREE, AND NUT-FREE

These help identify safe recipes for people with diet restrictions.

FREEZER FRIENDLY

Some smoothies don't work as well when they're frozen and thawed, especially if they have ice cubes in them. As you look through the cookbook, any recipe that's marked "Freezer Friendly" means it's a good one to freeze and enjoy later. Just pour it into ice cube trays, freeze, and enjoy it another time! When you're ready to have it, just add a little water (¼ to ½ cup) and blend it again until smooth.

Smoothies

Mighty Green Machine

DAIRY-FREE (DEPENDING ON MILK USED) · GLUTEN-FREE · NUT-FREE

PREP TIME
15 MINUTES

YIELD
1 OR 2 SERVINGS

WHAT YOU'LL NEED

½ cup frozen pineapple chunks

½ cup frozen mango chunks

1 cup milk of choice

½ cup fresh spinach

1 banana

1 teaspoon honey

I have a special connection to this recipe, so I'm making it the first recipe in the book! I used to make it for my kids every day before school. We've made this smoothie so many times that we could do it in our sleep! Now you, too, can power up your day with the delicious Mighty Green Machine!

1. **thaw** Take the frozen pineapple and mango out of the freezer and let it thaw on the counter for 5 minutes.

2. **add + blend** Add the milk to your blender. Add the spinach. Put the lid on the blender and blend for 1 full minute until the spinach is completely blended and smooth.

3. **peel + plop + add + blend** Peel the banana and plop it into the blender. Add the pineapple, mango, and honey. Put the lid on the blender and blend again.

4. **pour + split** Pour the smoothie into glasses and *banana-split it* with a friend!

TIP Try this smoothie with vanilla almond milk. Speaking of vanilla, do you know that vanilla can make things taste sweeter than they really are? If you want to make something taste a little sweeter without adding sugar, try a splash of vanilla extract instead!

Why is kale never lonely? Because it comes in bunches!

Winter Wonderland Gingerbread Spice

DAIRY-FREE (DEPENDING ON MILK USED AND WITHOUT WHIPPED CREAM) · GLUTEN-FREE · NUT-FREE

PREP TIME
20 MINUTES

YIELD
1 OR 2 SERVINGS

WHAT YOU'LL NEED

Warm water

¼ cup rolled oats

1 apple

1 banana

1 cup milk of choice

1½ teaspoons molasses (like unsulfured blackstrap molasses) or honey

½ teaspoon vanilla extract

¾ teaspoon ground cinnamon (or pumpkin pie spice) + more for sprinkling

1 cup ice cubes

Homemade Whipped Cream, for topping (see page 76; optional)

This recipe tastes like a gingerbread cookie, thanks to the spices, oats, and yummy molasses. The apples make it even tastier! You don't have to peel the apple—the skin is packed with nutrients that fight off germs.

1. **pour + soak** Pour the oats into a small bowl of warm water and let them soak for about 10 minutes. While they're soaking, move to the next step.

2. **chop + peel + drop** Chop the apple (ask an adult for help, if needed) and remove any seeds. Peel the banana and drop half into the blender (snack on the other half!) with the apple pieces.

3. **add + drain + add** Add the milk, molasses, vanilla, and cinnamon. Use a fine-mesh strainer to drain the soaked oats. Add the oats to the blender. Add the ice.

4. **blend + pour** Put the lid on the blender and blend until smooth and creamy. Pour the smoothie into glasses.

5. **garnish** Plop a dollop of whipped cream on top and sprinkle on some cinnamon.

TIP Cutting apples can get a bit DICEY because they can wobble. Ask an adult to slice them in half for you. Then, place the apple halves flat-side down on your cutting board. Chop away, master chef!

Pear-O-Saurus Smoothie

GLUTEN-FREE · NUT-FREE

PREP TIME
15 MINUTES

YIELD
1 OR 2 SERVINGS

WHAT YOU'LL NEED

1½ cups milk + more for thinning

1 big handful of spinach or kale

1 pear

1 banana

1 cup ice cubes

Pinch of ground nutmeg

Honey, for sweetening (optional)

What did the dinosaur say when it first tried a pear? "This is dino-mite! I just found my new favorite fruit!"

Banana makes this smoothie extra smooth and yummy, and spinach makes it green—though you can't really taste it! The pears have fiber, which helps you feel full and is good for digestion. Put 'em together, and it's Pear-O-Saurus perfection!

1. **splash + add + blend** Splash the milk into the blender. Add the spinach. Put the lid on the blender and blend for 1 minute. The liquid will be bright green.

2. **cut + add** Cut the pear into small pieces (ask an adult for help, if needed) and remove any seeds. Peel the banana and add the banana and pear pieces to the mix in the blender.

3. **add + pinch** Add the ice, along with a pinch of nutmeg.

4. **blend + taste + adjust** Put the lid on the blender and blend until smooth. If it seems too thick, add a little milk. Taste it. Does it need to be sweeter? Add some honey.

5. **pour + enjoy** Pour your Pear-O-Saurus into glasses, let out a big ROAR, and enjoy!

TIP Do you know that you can peel a banana from the non-stem side? Turn the banana upside down so the stem is at the bottom. Using your thumb and index finger, gently pinch the bump at the top of the banana. When the skin begins to split, pull it away from the fruit. *Ta-da!*

The Bees' Knees

5 INGREDIENT · GLUTEN-FREE · NUT-FREE

PREP TIME
15 MINUTES

YIELD
1 OR 2 SERVINGS

WHAT YOU'LL NEED

1 lemon + more to taste

1 cup milk

½ cup heavy whipping cream

2 tablespoons honey

½ cup ice cubes

In Greek mythology, honey was a special food of the gods that was often served at banquets on Mount Olympus. But you can make this yummy lemon-honey whipped cream smoothie anytime! It tastes sweet and tangy, like a lemon creamsicle, and the yellow color of the lemon makes the smoothie look bright and sunny, like a glass of sunshine!

1. **zest + squeeze + pour** Use a grater or zester to scrape off the yellow outer layer of the lemon, not the bitter white part. Add the zest to the blender. Cut the lemon in half (ask an adult for help, if needed). Squeeze the juice from one half into a small bowl, remove any seeds, and pour the juice into the blender. Add a little more lemon juice from the other half (squeezing it into the bowl first and removing any seeds) if you like it really lemony!

2. **add** Add the milk, heavy cream, and honey.

3. **blend + add + pour** Put the lid on the blender and blend until well combined. Add the ice, put the lid on again, and blend until smooth. Pour the smoothie into glasses and share it around—soon everyone will be buzzing about it!

TIP To get more juice from your lemon, roll it firmly on a hard surface (like a table or countertop) before cutting it open.

What kind of bee can't be understood? A mumble bee!

Pumpkin Pie Smoothie

GLUTEN-FREE · NUT-FREE

PREP TIME
15 MINUTES

YIELD
1 OR 2 SERVINGS

WHAT YOU'LL NEED

1 banana

1 cup milk

⅓ cup pumpkin puree

½ teaspoon vanilla extract

¼ teaspoon ground cinnamon + more for sprinkling

1 tablespoon pure maple syrup + more to taste

½ cup ice cubes

Homemade Whipped Cream, for topping (see page 76; optional)

Imagine taking the best flavors of pumpkin pie and blending them into a delicious drink—it's like autumn in a glass! Pumpkins are an excellent source of vitamin A. Vitamin A helps your eyes work better, especially in the dark.

1. **peel + toss + add** Peel the banana and toss it into the blender. Add the milk and pumpkin puree. Add the vanilla and cinnamon. Add the maple syrup and ice.

2. **blend + taste + adjust** Put the lid on the blender and blend until smooth. Have a taste! Does it need to be sweeter? Add a little more maple syrup.

3. **pour + top** Pour your smoothie into glasses. Top with a plop of whipped cream, if you like, and cozy up with this smoothie for the full pumpkin pie experience—yum!

TIP If you have pumpkin pie spice, try this instead of cinnamon. Pumpkin pie spice is a blend of ingredients (including cinnamon) that really brings out the yummy seasonal flavors in this smoothie!

Who helps the little pumpkins cross the road to school? *The Crossing Gourd!*

Banana Coconut Sundae Shake

5 INGREDIENT · DAIRY-FREE · GLUTEN-FREE

PREP TIME
15 MINUTES

YIELD
1 OR 2 SERVINGS

WHAT YOU'LL NEED

1 banana

1 cup full-fat coconut milk

2 tablespoons unsweetened cocoa powder

1 tablespoon honey

1 cup ice cubes

Dried coconut, for topping (optional)

This chocolate smoothie is perfect for when you want something sweet and chocolatey! It tastes like dessert, but it's made from natural ingredients. Also, you need only four ingredients to make it (okay, five if you count the ice!).

1. **peel + drop + add + blend** Peel the banana and drop it into the blender. Add the coconut milk, cocoa powder, honey, and ice. Put the lid on the blender and blend, blend, blend!

2. **pour + sprinkle** Pour the smoothie into glasses, sprinkle the top with dried coconut, if you wish, and enjoy.

TIP Instead of using honey in this recipe, you can use 1 tablespoon of pure maple syrup, agave nectar, or sugar!

What kind of key opens a banana? A mon-key!

Orange Blossom Oasis

GLUTEN-FREE · NUT-FREE

PREP TIME
15 MINUTES

YIELD
1 OR 2 SERVINGS

WHAT YOU'LL NEED

¾ cup plain yogurt

½ cup orange juice

1 orange, peeled + broken into pieces

½ cup cold water

½ cup ice cubes

1 big pinch of ground turmeric

Honey to taste (optional)

This yummy drink is inspired by the flavors of Lebanon, a beautiful subtropical nation in the Middle East that grows citrus fruits. The Orange Blossom Oasis is tangy and refreshing. And don't forget to add the turmeric—that's what gives this drink its beautiful orange color.

1. **chuck** Chuck the yogurt and the orange juice into the blender. Add the orange pieces. Add the cold water, ice, and turmeric.

2. **blend + taste + add** Put the lid on the blender and blend until super smooth. Taste your drink. Does it need to be sweeter? If so, add a drizzle of honey, then cover the blender again and blend it in.

3. **pour + cheers** Pour the smoothie into glasses, and announce, "*fi sih-TUK!*" (That's "cheers" in Arabic, the official language of Lebanon.)

TIP Cleanup in the kitchen can be boring, so here's a fun trick for cleaning your blender: Right after you finish using it, fill it halfway with warm water and a drop of dish soap. Put the lid back on and blend for 30 seconds to loosen all the food residue. Pour out the soapy water and rinse the blender with warm water. Nice work!

Have you heard that nothing rhymes with orange? It doesn't.

What do you get when you mix dragons and cocoa powder? Dragon hot chocolate, of course! It's the perfect drink for a fire-breathing dragon on a chilly day.

Dragon's Lair Cocoa Smoothie

GLUTEN-FREE · NUT-FREE

PREP TIME
15 MINUTES

YIELD
1 OR 2 SERVINGS

WHAT YOU'LL NEED

Warm water

2 dates (without pits)

½ banana

½ avocado, peeled and pitted (see Tip)

1 cup milk

2 tablespoons unsweetened cocoa powder

1 cup ice cubes

Handful of chocolate chips + more for sprinkling

What do you get when you blend creamy avocado, sweet banana, and CHOCOLATE? A super-tasty drink that tastes a lot like a chocolate-covered banana! It's so tasty, in fact, that you'll want to sneak off and hide somewhere to drink it all yourself—like a dragon in their lair!

1. **soak + drain + chop + add** Fill a small bowl with warm tap water, add the dates, and let them soak for 10 to 15 minutes to soften them. Drain the water and chop up the dates (ask an adult for help, if needed). Add the dates to the blender.

2. **peel + chuck + add** Peel the banana half and chuck it into the blender along with the avocado. Add the milk, cocoa powder, and ice.

3. **blend + sprinkle + pour + top** Put the lid on the blender and blend everything together. Sprinkle in the chocolate chips, put the lid back on, and blend again until creamy and thick.

4. **pour + sprinkle + enjoy!** Pour the smoothie into glasses, sprinkle chocolate chips on top, and enjoy!

TIP Removing an avocado pit can be tricky, so do it safely and ask an adult for help, if needed (see "How to Prep an Avocado," page 28).

Sweet Pea Green Goblin

GLUTEN-FREE · NUT-FREE

PREP TIME
15 MINUTES

YIELD
1 OR 2 SERVINGS

WHAT YOU'LL NEED

1 cup milk

½ cup water

1½ frozen bananas
(see Tip)

⅓ cup frozen peas

2 tablespoons
unsweetened cocoa
powder (or a handful of
chocolate chips)

1 tablespoon honey +
more to taste

1 fresh mint leaf (or a
basil leaf or a drop of
peppermint extract)

Peas in a smoothie? Trust us, it's no joke! You won't really taste the peas—only the bananas, creamy chocolate, and minty sweetness; in fact, you'll be GOBLIN' it up in no time! Green peas are a good source of protein, and protein helps you grow strong cells, bones, and muscles.

1. **pour + add** Pour the milk and water into the blender. Add the bananas, peas, cocoa powder, and honey.

2. **tear + blend + pour** Tear up a mint leaf and add it to the blender. Put the lid on the blender and blend until smooth and thick. Pour the smoothie into glasses, and serve with big straws.

TIP If you need to freeze bananas quickly, peel them, chop them into small bits, place them on a plate, and stick them in the freezer for about 20 minutes.

What do polite vegetables always say? Peas to meet you!

Vanilla Bean Dream Delight

5 INGREDIENT · GLUTEN-FREE · NUT-FREE

PREP TIME
15 MINUTES

YIELD
1 OR 2 SERVINGS

WHAT YOU'LL NEED

1 banana

3 tablespoons canned white beans

½ cup Greek yogurt (plain or vanilla)

1 teaspoon vanilla extract

2 tablespoons honey

1 cup ice cubes

We named this creamy, dreamy, beany smoothie a "bean dream delight" smoothie for two reasons: First, it contains white beans. Second, it contains vanilla, which comes from a vanilla BEAN! It may sound weird to put white beans in a smoothie, but they add a ton of creaminess. So, give it a whirl and see if anyone can guess your secret ingredient!

1. **peel + plop** Peel the banana and plop it into your blender.

2. **add** Add the white beans, yogurt, vanilla, honey, and ice.

3. **blend + pour + enjoy** Put the lid on the blender and blend the smoothie until creamy and thick. Pour the smoothie into glasses, and enjoy with a friend—can they guess the mystery ingredient?!

 TIP For an equally tasty smoothie, swap the white beans for 3 tablespoons of nut butter.

What bean is the most intelligent? The human bean!

TIP Are your bananas still green? It might mean they aren't quite ripe yet, but no problem! Place them in a brown paper bag and close the top. Let your bananas hang out there for at least 24 hours. Bananas release a gas called ethylene that helps them ripen and sweeten, and trapping this gas inside the bag with the bananas speeds up this process.

Tres Amigas Avocado Batido

DAIRY-FREE · GLUTEN-FREE · NUT-FREE

PREP TIME
15 MINUTES

YIELD
1 OR 2 SERVINGS

WHAT YOU'LL NEED

1 avocado

1 banana

1 handful of fresh or frozen spinach

1 lime (for juicing)

1 cup full-fat coconut milk

¼ cup water + more if needed

½ cup ice cubes

Honey to taste (optional)

Mmmmmmm, sweet banana, creamy coconut, buttery avocado—this shake, or batido (*ba-TEE-doh*) in Spanish, is full of nutrients to give you lots of energy. And after just one sip, you'll be transported to the tropics of Mexico. Close your eyes and imagine the palm trees swaying in the warm breeze!

1. **slice + twist + scoop** Using a butter knife or safety knife, carefully slice the avocado around its pit lengthwise. Twist each half to open it. Remove the pit (ask an adult for help, if needed; see "How to Prep an Avocado," page 28). With a spoon, scoop the avocado from its shell and into your blender.

2. **peel + add + cut + squeeze** Peel the banana and toss it into your blender. Add the spinach. Cut the lime in half (ask an adult for help, if needed). Squeeze the juice from both halves into a small bowl and pour the juice into the blender.

3. **add + blend + adjust** Add the coconut milk and water. Add the ice. Put the lid on the blender and blend until smooth. If the milk shake seems too thick, blend in a little water. If it needs sweetening, add a little honey.

4. **pour + cheers** Pour the smoothie into glasses, and shout, "*sa-LOOD!*" (That's "cheers" in Spanish.)

Downside-Up Pineapple Smoothie

GLUTEN-FREE · NUT-FREE

PREP TIME
15 MINUTES

YIELD
1 OR 2 SERVINGS

WHAT YOU'LL NEED

½ cup pineapple chunks (canned, fresh, or frozen)

1 cup milk

½ teaspoon vanilla extract

1 banana

½ cup ice cubes

Honey to taste (optional)

1 or 2 Maraschino cherries (optional)

Have you ever had pineapple upside-down cake? Well, today we're flipping things around with a blender mashup that tastes just like pineapple upside-down cake. And sure, pineapples are sweet and delicious, but they also fight inflammation and pain and help your body digest food.

1. **toss + peel + add** Toss the pineapple into your blender. Add the milk and vanilla. Peel the banana and add it to the blender. Add the ice.

2. **blend + taste + adjust** Put the lid on the blender and blend until smooth. Taste it. Does it taste too sour? If so, blend in a little honey.

3. **pour + top** Pour the smoothie into glasses, and top off with a Maraschino cherry—YUM!

TIP Feel free to use fresh cherries in place of the Maraschino cherries.

When is an apple not an apple? When it's a pineapple!

Nectar of the Gods

5 INGREDIENT · GLUTEN-FREE · NUT-FREE

PREP TIME
15 MINUTES

YIELD
1 OR 2 SERVINGS

WHAT YOU'LL NEED

1 orange

½ cup apple juice

½ cup plain yogurt

½ cup cold water

1 cup ice cubes (optional)

Mini marshmallows, for topping (optional)

In ancient Greek mythology, ambrosia was the food of the gods. It was said that anyone who consumed it would live forever. In cooking, ambrosia is a fruity, juicy dessert made from oranges and coconut. In addition to being delicious, it's nutritious! The vitamins in oranges heal cuts and scrapes and help your skin feel and look smooth.

1. **cut + squeeze** Cut the orange in half (ask an adult for help, if needed). Squeeze the juice from both halves into a small bowl, remove any seeds, and pour the juice into your blender.

2. **add** Add the apple juice and yogurt.

3. **blend** Put the lid on the blender and blend until smooth. Add the cold water, put the lid on again, and blend. If you want a thicker shake, blend in the ice.

4. **pour + sprinkle + enjoy** Pour the shake into glasses. Sprinkle with mini marshmallows, if desired. Enjoy!

TIP Use any type of orange, like mandarin oranges, tangerines, or two clementine oranges (because they're small).

What's a vampire's favorite smoothie?
"Neck-tar of the gods," of course!

Very Berry Zest Quest

GLUTEN-FREE · NUT-FREE

PREP TIME
15 MINUTES

YIELD
1 OR 2 SERVINGS

WHAT YOU'LL NEED

¼ cup chopped fresh zucchini

½ lemon

¼ cup frozen blueberries

1 cup milk

1½ frozen bananas

1 teaspoon honey + more for drizzling

We're on a quest for zest, and you may be surprised that it involves a zucchini! But to be clear, the flavor in this drink comes from the juicy berries and creamy banana, the tart lemon and sweet honey. You can thank the zucchini for adding creaminess and heart-healthy potassium, without adding any flavor. How's that for sneaky?!

1. **toss + squeeze + pour** Toss the zucchini into your blender. Squeeze the juice from the lemon half into a small bowl, remove any seeds, and pour the juice into your blender.

2. **add** Add the blueberries and milk to the blender. Then add the frozen bananas and honey.

3. **blend + drizzle + sip** Put the lid on the blender and blend until smooth and dreamy! Pour the smoothie into glasses, and drizzle with honey. Sip, sip, hooray!

TIP For an extra creamy smoothie, chop the zucchini into pieces first, then freeze it!

What did the blueberry say to the lemon?
"You're my zest friend!"

Heart Beet Smoothie

GLUTEN-FREE · NUT-FREE

PREP TIME
15 MINUTES

YIELD
1 OR 2 SERVINGS

WHAT YOU'LL NEED

1 or 2 bananas

½ cup milk

¼ cup beets (canned or fresh cooked and cooled; not pickled; or frozen cherries)

1 cup fresh or frozen berries

½ cup plain yogurt

1 tablespoon honey + more to taste

Fresh raspberries, pomegranate seeds, or other fresh fruit, for topping (optional)

When your friends and family see this beautiful, bright-pink smoothie, they might wonder if you made it with fairy dust. Imagine their surprise when you reveal the magic ingredient: BEETS!

Beets contain lots of iron, which helps you stay healthy and gives you energy.

1. **peel + add** Peel the bananas and add them to the blender. Add the milk, beets, and berries. Add the yogurt and honey.

2. **blend + pour + top** Put the lid on the blender and blend until smooth and creamy. Pour the smoothie into glasses, and top with raspberries or pomegranate seeds, if you want more pink power!

TIP Consider wearing latex gloves when you're working with beets (and pomegranate seeds)—they'll prevent your hands from getting stained pink. Also, beets are slippery, and gloves make them easier to grip.

What do you call a happy vegetable?
UpBeet!

Cheerful Cherry Pie

DAIRY-FREE (DEPENDING ON MILK USED) · GLUTEN-FREE

PREP TIME
15 MINUTES

YIELD
1 OR 2 SERVINGS

WHAT YOU'LL NEED

½ cup milk of choice (almond milk is good here)

¼ cup almond flour (optional)

½ banana

1 cup frozen cherries

1 handful of dried cherries (or another dried fruit like cranberries or raisins)

1 fresh peach, halved and pitted

1 teaspoon honey

½ teaspoon almond or vanilla extract (optional)

Pinch of salt

Cherries are in season in summer—that's why cherry pies appear at picnics and barbecues. Did you know that a single cherry tree can produce up to 100 pounds of cherries per year? Use some of those cherries to make this delicious summer smoothie that includes another summer favorite—peaches!

1. **place + blend** Place the milk and almond flour in your blender. Put the lid on the blender and blend until smooth.

2. **peel + add** Peel the banana and add half to the blender (see Tip). Add the frozen and dried cherries. Add the peach halves and honey. Add the almond extract (if using) and salt.

3. **blend + pour + enjoy** Put the lid on the blender and blend until smooth and creamy. Pour the smoothie into glasses, and enjoy your cherry-licious concoction!

TIP Anytime you have leftover banana, like here (or bananas that are getting overripe), pop them into a freezer bag and freeze for future smoothies. This goes for any fruit that's looking kind of tired!

What do cherries say to their best friends? "You're cherrific!"

Double Coconut Crusher

5 INGREDIENT · DAIRY-FREE · GLUTEN-FREE · NUT-FREE

PREP TIME
15 MINUTES

YIELD
1 OR 2 SERVINGS

WHAT YOU'LL NEED

Warm water

2 dates (without pits)

1 banana

1 cup full-fat coconut milk

1 tablespoon sweetened dried shredded coconut + more for sprinkling

1½ teaspoons lemon juice

1 to 1½ cups ice cubes

This creamy, tasty smoothie plays off the flavors of the classic macaroon, a small, thick cookie typically made from coconut and condensed milk. It's basically the drinkable version, and it's yummy and good for you, too! The coconut milk contains electrolytes, which prevent dehydration and help sore muscles. Take this smoothie on the go and run with it!

1. **soak + drain + chop + add** Fill a small bowl with warm tap water, add the dates, and let soak for 10 to 15 minutes to soften them. Drain the water and chop up the dates (ask an adult for help, if needed). Add the dates to the blender.

2. **peel + add** Peel the banana and add it to your blender.

3. **add** Add the coconut milk, shredded coconut, lemon juice, and ice (the more ice you add, the thicker your smoothie will be).

4. **blend + pour + sprinkle** Put the lid on the blender and blend until creamy and thick. Pour the smoothie into glasses, sprinkle with shredded coconut, and get ready to crush your thirst!

TIP Instead of using dried coconut to top this smoothie, try grated apple—yum!

What do you call a fruit that goes into space? A coco-naut!

PB&J Twist

GLUTEN-FREE (WITHOUT TOPPING)

PREP TIME
15 MINUTES

YIELD
1 OR 2 SERVINGS

WHAT YOU'LL NEED

1 banana

1 cup milk

1 cup frozen strawberries

2 tablespoons
strawberry jam

¼ cup peanut butter

Crushed graham crackers
or pretzels,
for topping (optional)

What's a PB&J that doesn't fit in your lunch box? A PB&J smoothie, of course! This fun twist on the famous lunch sandwich will wow you with its creamy sweetness that combines a PB&J with peanut butter and banana—all drinkable with a straw! Peanut butter is high in protein and healthy fats, so it tastes great and fuels your day—zoom, zoom!

1. **peel + add** Peel the banana and add it to your blender. Add the milk, strawberries, strawberry jam, and peanut butter.

2. **blend + pour + top** Put the lid on the blender and blend until smooth. Pour the smoothie into glasses, and top with crushed graham crackers or pretzels, if you'd like.

TIP   Chocolate-covered pretzels or graham crackers are also DELICIOUS in this recipe!

What do you call a peanut who goes into outer space? An astro-nut!

Carrot Cake Shake-Up

GLUTEN-FREE

PREP TIME
15 MINUTES

YIELD
1 OR 2 SERVINGS

WHAT YOU'LL NEED

FOR THE SMOOTHIE:

1 frozen banana

½ cup apple juice

1 carrot

½ cup frozen pineapple chunks

2 tablespoons granola

2 teaspoons honey

2 pinches of ground cinnamon or pumpkin pie spice

Homemade Whipped Cream, for topping (recipe follows; optional)

FOR THE HOMEMADE WHIPPED CREAM (OPTIONAL):

1 or 2 cups heavy whipping cream

Squeeze of lemon juice

1 tablespoon pure maple syrup

Pinch of salt

Carrots contain more sugar than most other vegetables and have been used to sweeten desserts throughout history. Carrots also come in a variety of colors, including purple, red, yellow, white, and, of course, orange. Any color carrot tastes great in this smoothie, so hop to it and see for yourself!

1. **thaw** Take a frozen banana out of the freezer and let it thaw on the counter for 5 minutes.

2. **add + shake** If you're making the Homemade Whipped Cream, fill a plastic jar halfway with the heavy cream. Add the lemon juice, maple syrup, and salt. Cover the jar and shake until the cream has thickened and stops sloshing around in the container. Set aside.

3. **add + grate + blend** Add the apple juice to the blender. Carefully grate the carrot (see "How to Grate a Carrot," page 29) and wing it into the blender. Put the lid on the blender and blend for 1 full minute.

4. **add + blend** Add the frozen pineapple to the mixture in the blender. Add the granola, honey, and cinnamon. Put the lid back on the blender and blend again until smooth.

5. **pour + plop** Pour the smoothie into glasses, and plop some whipped cream on top, if you like. It's like having your cake and drinking it, too!

How do you know carrots are good for your eyes? Well, have you ever seen a rabbit wearing glasses?

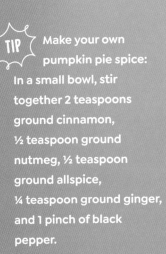

TIP Make your own pumpkin pie spice: In a small bowl, stir together 2 teaspoons ground cinnamon, ½ teaspoon ground nutmeg, ½ teaspoon ground allspice, ¼ teaspoon ground ginger, and 1 pinch of black pepper.

Pineappley Cheesecakey-Shakey

5 INGREDIENT · GLUTEN-FREE (WITHOUT GRAHAM CRACKER) · NUT-FREE

PREP TIME
15 MINUTES

YIELD
1 OR 2 SERVINGS

WHAT YOU'LL NEED

½ cup whole milk

2 tablespoons cream cheese, softened

½ cup frozen pineapple chunks

1½ teaspoons honey

½ cup ice cubes

1 graham cracker (optional)

This sweet, tangy, impossibly creamy smoothie is inspired by a popular dessert called New York–style cheesecake. It even has a sprinkle of graham cracker, just like the crust of the cheesecake. And here's a fun fact: Pineapples were originally called "*anana*" in the Caribbean, which means "excellent fruit." We think pineapples are pretty amazing, too!

1. **sling** Sling the milk and cream cheese into your blender. Add the pineapple and honey.

2. **add + blend + pour** Add the ice, put the lid on the blender, and blend until smooth. Pour the smoothie into glasses.

3. **crush + sprinkle** If you wish, place the graham cracker in a resealable plastic bag, seal it closed, and crush it with your hands until it breaks up into crumbs. Sprinkle the crumbs on top and enjoy!

TIP For a nondairy option, replace the cream cheese with ½ frozen banana, and the whole milk with a full-fat nondairy milk, like full-fat coconut milk.

How do you compliment a pineapple? Call it a fine-apple.

Banana Dulce de Leche

DAIRY-FREE · GLUTEN-FREE · NUT-FREE

PREP TIME
20 MINUTES

YIELD
1 OR 2 SERVINGS

WHAT YOU'LL NEED

Warm water

3 dates (without pits)

1 frozen banana

1 cup full-fat coconut milk

½ teaspoon vanilla extract

Juice of ½ orange

Pinch of salt

"Dulce de leche" (*DOHL-say-day-LAY-chay*) is Spanish for "sweet milk" or "milk candy." Dulce de leche tastes a lot like caramel and is often used in the same way— as a filling in cookies or a topping on ice cream. It's a special treat enjoyed throughout Latin and South America. Enjoy this nutrient-packed version in smoothie form!

1. **soak + drain + add** Fill a small bowl with warm tap water, add the dates, and let soak for 10 to 15 minutes to soften them. Drain the water and add the dates to the blender.

2. **thaw** Take the banana out of the freezer and let it thaw on the counter for 5 minutes.

3. **add** Add the coconut milk and vanilla to the blender.

4. **pour + add** Pour the orange juice into the blender. Add the salt and banana.

5. **blend + pour** Put the lid on the blender and blend until smooth and creamy. Pour the smoothie into glasses. *Delicioso!*

TIP Dates are so sweet that they are sometimes known as "nature's candy"!

What's the best thing to put in a banana smoothie? A straw!

Turkish Delight Smoothie

GLUTEN-FREE · NUT-FREE

PREP TIME
20 MINUTES

YIELD
1 OR 2 SERVINGS

WHAT YOU'LL NEED

Warm water

1 handful of dried apricots

1 frozen banana

1 cup orange juice

½ cup yogurt

1 tablespoon honey
+ more to taste

1 teaspoon vanilla extract

Dash of ground cinnamon

Dash of ground nutmeg

This smoothie is inspired by the fruity flavors of a gummy candy that's popular in parts of Europe and the Middle East and known as Turkish Delight. Its soft, squishy, sticky texture is often dusted with powdered sugar and comes in different colors and fruity flavors, like apricot, orange, and pomegranate. When you taste this smoothie, you'll understand what the fruity hype's all about!

1. **soak + drain + add** Fill a small bowl with warm tap water, add the dried apricots, and let soak for 10 to 15 minutes to soften them. Drain the water and add the apricots to the blender.

2. **thaw** Take the banana out of the freezer and let it thaw on the counter for 5 minutes.

3. **drop** Drop the banana, orange juice, yogurt, honey, vanilla, cinnamon, and nutmeg into the blender.

4. **blend + pour + cheers** Put the lid on the blender and blend until smooth and creamy. Pour the smoothie into glasses, and say "cheers" in Turkish—"şerefe!" (*CHE-reh-feh*).

TIP If you don't have nutmeg, use more cinnamon.

Why did the orange stop at the top of the hill? Because it ran out of juice!

Banana Berrylicious

GLUTEN-FREE · NUT-FREE

PREP TIME
15 MINUTES

YIELD
1 OR 2 SERVINGS

WHAT YOU'LL NEED

1 cup milk

½ cup plain yogurt

1 banana

1 orange

½ cup frozen berries of choice

1 cup ice cubes

1 teaspoon honey, agave nectar, or stevia (a natural sweetener) + more to taste

Did you know that honey never spoils? When King Tut's tomb was discovered in 1922, jars of honey were included with his treasures. Even though the honey was more than 3,000 years old, it was still edible! Enjoy your fresh honey with berries, orange, and banana in this sweet treat!

1. **add** Add the milk and yogurt to your blender.

2. **peel + cut + squeeze** Peel the banana and add it to the blender. Cut the orange in half (ask an adult for help, if needed). Squeeze the juice from one half into a bowl (save the other half for a tasty snack), remove any seeds, and pour the juice into the blender.

3. **add** Add the berries and ice. Add the honey.

4. **blend + taste + adjust** Put the lid on the blender and blend until smooth. Taste it. If you want it sweeter, drizzle in more honey, put the lid on the blender, and blend again.

5. **pour + enjoy** Pour the smoothie into glasses and enjoy!

TIP Have you ever tried honey powder? It's a great sweetener and reduces the stickiness you get with honey. You can sprinkle it on top of this or any smoothie for added *oomf*! Look for it online.

What would you call two banana skins? A pair of slippers.

Milk Tea Tango

5 INGREDIENT · GLUTEN-FREE · NUT-FREE

PREP TIME
30 MINUTES

YIELD
1 OR 2 SERVINGS

WHAT YOU'LL NEED

1 cup whole milk

2 decaffeinated green tea bags

1 frozen banana

½ cup whole-milk vanilla yogurt

1 tablespoon honey + more to taste

Do you enjoy boba tea? If so, you'll definitely want to try this yummy, creamy milk smoothie made with green tea. Even though it's a sweet treat, the ingredients are nutritious and energy-boosting, and the green tea is known to keep you healthy!

1. **steep** Pour the milk into a bowl. Add the tea bags to the milk, stir, and leave the tea bags to sit in the milk for 20 to 30 minutes. (Go do something fun!)

2. **thaw** Take the frozen banana out of the freezer and let it thaw on the counter for 5 minutes.

3. **toss + pour + blend** Toss the banana, yogurt, and honey into your blender. Once the tea is done steeping in the milk, remove the tea bags and pour the milk tea into the blender. Put the lid on the blender and blend until smooth.

4. **taste + adjust + pour** Taste the smoothie. Does it need more sweetness? If so, blend in a bit more honey. Pour the smoothie into glasses and enjoy!

TIP If you don't have any frozen bananas, use ½ banana + a few ice cubes, or follow the tip on page 60 to flash freeze your bananas.

Where do milk shakes come from? Nervous cows.

Pineapple Paradise

DAIRY-FREE · GLUTEN-FREE · NUT-FREE

PREP TIME
15 MINUTES

YIELD
1 OR 2 SERVINGS

WHAT YOU'LL NEED

½ cup full-fat coconut milk

¼ cup orange juice + more if needed

½ cup fresh spinach leaves

1¼ cups frozen pineapple chunks

2 teaspoons honey (or pure maple syrup)

1 teaspoon grated fresh ginger

Pineapple is native to South America, and ginger is native to Southeast Asia. But today, both are grown in many tropical regions. Sometimes there's a sticker on the fruit telling you where it's from. This drinkable treat will leave you imagining that you're in a tropical paradise, picking the fruit off the tree yourself!

1. **pour + add + blend** Pour the coconut milk and orange juice into your blender. Add the spinach. Put the lid on the blender and blend for 1 full minute until the spinach is completely blended and smooth.

2. **add** Add the frozen pineapple, honey, and ginger.

3. **blend + pour** Put the lid on the blender and blend until smooth and creamy. If the mixture is too thick, add a splash more orange juice to thin it out. Blend it again, then pour the smoothie into glasses, and take a trip to paradise!

TIP Whenever you make a smoothie with greens, like spinach or kale, start by blending the greens with the liquid for 1 full minute. This makes it really smooth.

Did you hear about the person who tried to make a pineapple smoothie without any pineapples? Their efforts were fruitless.

Brownie Batter Smoothie

DAIRY-FREE (DEPENDING ON MILK USED) · GLUTEN-FREE

PREP TIME
20 MINUTES

YIELD
1 OR 2 SERVINGS

WHAT YOU'LL NEED

Warm water

4 or 5 dates (without pits)

½ cup milk of choice

½ cup canned pumpkin

¼ cup silken tofu
(or a banana)

2 tablespoons nut butter

¼ cup unsweetened
cocoa powder

¼ teaspoon vanilla extract

½ cup ice cubes

Imagine starting your day with a smoothie that tastes like a brownie and is packed with nutrients that give you all the energy you need for the day. It's like having dessert for breakfast, and it's so nutritious, grown-ups won't give you a hard time about it—they may even ask for some!

1. **soak + drain + add** Fill a small bowl with warm tap water, add the dates, and let soak for 10 to 15 minutes to soften them. Drain the water and add the dates to the blender.

2. **add** Add the milk, pumpkin, tofu, nut butter, cocoa powder, and vanilla to the blender. Add the ice cubes.

3. **blend + pour** Put the lid on the blender and blend until smooth and creamy. Pour the smoothie into glasses and enjoy!

TIP For a tasty twist to your drinks, try freezing juice, fruit puree, herbal tea, or coconut milk into ice cubes. Then, add them to your favorite drinks and smoothies for a flavorful boost. Grab an ice cube tray and get creative with your own custom ice cubes!

"Knock, knock!" "Who's there?" "Bean." "Bean who?" "It's Bean a while since I had a brownie, hand it over!"

Jicama Fiesta Slushie

5 INGREDIENT · DAIRY-FREE · GLUTEN-FREE · NUT-FREE

PREP TIME
15 MINUTES

YIELD
1 OR 2 SERVINGS

WHAT YOU'LL NEED

1 lime

¼ cup honey

1 cup water

Pinch of salt

¼ cup chopped peeled jicama

1½ cups ice cubes

Jicama is a really cool and funny-looking vegetable. It looks like a big, brown potato on the outside, but the inside is crunchy and refreshing. Some people think it looks like a cross between an apple and a pear. Jicama is usually eaten raw as a snack or in salads (and sometimes in smoothies!).

● ● ● ● ● ● ● ● ● ● ● ● ● ● ● ● ● ●

1. **cut + peel** Cut the lime into 4 wedges (ask an adult for help, if needed). Remove the peel and excess white pith from each wedge.

2. **add** Add the lime wedges, honey, water, and salt to the blender.

3. **peel + chop + add** With the help of an adult, peel and chop the jicama. Add it to the blender. Add the ice.

4. **blend + pour** Put the lid on the blender and blend until smooth and creamy. Pour the smoothie into glasses and enjoy!

TIP If you can't find jicama, try a green apple or a pear instead.

What could you say to your friend if they spilled their slushie? "Don't worry, FREEZE things happen!"

Totally Tropicool Fruit Smoothie

5 INGREDIENT · DAIRY-FREE · GLUTEN-FREE · NUT-FREE

PREP TIME
15 MINUTES

YIELD
1 OR 2 SERVINGS

WHAT YOU'LL NEED

1 frozen banana

½ (13-ounce) can full-fat coconut milk

1 lime (for juicing)

Pinch of ground nutmeg

Pinch of ground ginger (optional)

The tropics are like a wild, colorful garden filled with amazing animals, like cheeky monkeys and vibrant birds. So it's no surprise that you'll find luscious fruits there, like the banana, coconut, and nutmeg we'll use in this totally tropical smoothie.

1. **thaw + shake + pour** Take the frozen banana out of the freezer and let it thaw on the counter for 5 minutes. Meanwhile, shake the can of coconut milk, carefully open it, and pour half of the contents into your blender.

2. **cut + squeeze + toss** Cut the lime in half (ask an adult for help, if needed). Squeeze the juice from both halves into a small bowl and pour the juice into the blender. Toss in the banana, nutmeg, and, if you wish, dried ginger.

3. **blend + pour** Put the lid on the blender and blend until smooth and creamy. Pour the smoothie into glasses and enjoy!

TIP How many tropical fruits can you think of? Any would taste great in this smoothie! Try frozen pineapple, mango, papaya, guava, passion fruit, or açaí!

Why did the bananas work at a smoothie shop? They wanted to blend in!

Raspberry Delight with Cocoa Drizzle

5 INGREDIENT · GLUTEN-FREE · NUT-FREE

PREP TIME
15 MINUTES

YIELD
1 OR 2 SERVINGS

WHAT YOU'LL NEED

FOR THE RASPBERRY DELIGHT:

1 cup plain Greek yogurt

1 cup frozen raspberries

½ teaspoon honey

1½ cups ice cubes

FOR THE COCOA DRIZZLE:

2 tablespoons Greek yogurt

½ teaspoon unsweetened cocoa powder

½ teaspoon honey

Did you know that raspberries are made up of lots of tiny fruits? They're called "drupelets," and each raspberry has around one hundred of them! Each drupelet has a little seed inside. When raspberries are ready to be picked, they come off the plant easily, but the stem stays behind. This makes a little hole in the middle of the raspberry where the stem used to be.

● ● ● ● ● ● ● ● ● ● ● ● ● ●

1. **add** Add the yogurt, raspberries, honey, and ice cubes to your blender.

2. **blend** Put the lid on the blender and blend until smooth and creamy.

3. **add + whisk** Put the yogurt in a small bowl. Add the cocoa powder and honey, and, using a whisk or fork, mix them together.

4. **pour + drizzle** Pour the smoothie into glasses, and, using a fork or whisk, drizzle the cocoa mixture on top!

TIP Make this a different berry delight by swapping the raspberries for blackberries, blueberries, or strawberries!

Raspberry and Milk met at a party. How were they introduced? "Raspberry, Milk, shake!"

Why did the lychee feel lucky?
Because it found its way into
this delicious recipe!

Lucky Lychee

5 INGREDIENT · DAIRY-FREE (DEPENDING ON MILK USED) · GLUTEN-FREE ·
NUT-FREE (DEPENDING ON MILK USED)

PREP TIME
15 MINUTES

YIELD
1 OR 2 SERVINGS

WHAT YOU'LL NEED

1 cup milk of choice +
more if needed

½ cup lychees in syrup

1 banana

½ cup frozen mango
chunks

Ever heard of a lychee? It's a small, round, tropical fruit, native to southern China. Lychees are said to bring heaps of good luck, so folks feast on them during the Lunar New Year holiday. They're the star of the show in desserts and drinks, like sorbet, bubble tea, and this smoothie. Look for lychees in the international aisle of the supermarket—they're usually sold in cans.

1. **add** Add the milk to your blender. Add the lychees, reserving the syrup.

2. **peel + add** Peel the banana and add half to the blender (eat or freeze the other half). Add the mango.

3. **blend + taste + adjust** Put the lid on the blender and blend until smooth. If it's too thick, add a bit more milk. Give it a taste. If it needs more sweetness, add a little lychee syrup. Put the lid on the blender again and blend until smooth.

4. **pour + cheers** Pour the smoothie into glasses, and yell out a big *"gānbēi"* (*gahn-BAY*)! That's "cheers" in Chinese. And then, bottoms up!

TIP If you can't find canned lychees in syrup, use mandarin oranges instead. And if you have leftover syrup from lychees, mandarins, or any canned fruit, pour it over fresh fruit—it's extra tasty on berries, peaches, or pineapple.

Enchanted Blackberry Fairy Frostie

GLUTEN-FREE

PREP TIME
15 MINUTES

YIELD
1 OR 2 SERVINGS

WHAT YOU'LL NEED

1 frozen banana

¼ cup frozen blackberries

1 tablespoon instant oats

½ cup milk

2 tablespoons plain yogurt

½ teaspoon vanilla extract

1½ teaspoons nut butter

1 teaspoon honey (or agave nectar)

1 lime (for zesting + juicing)

According to the lore and tales of old,
a blackberry's worth its weight in gold!
Purple, yellow, black, or red—
don't like one color? Pick another instead!
We fairies know one thing is true:
Blackberries are very good for you.
Welsh legend says when you eat a blackberry,
a fairy may appear (goodness, how merry!).
So, make this frostie, and pour it in a cup,
a magical potion for you to drink up!

1. **thaw** Take the frozen banana and blackberries out of the freezer and let them thaw on the counter for 5 enchanting minutes.

2. **add** Add the oats, milk, yogurt, vanilla, nut butter, honey, banana, and berries to your blender.

3. **zest + squeeze + pour** Use a grater or zester to scrape off the green outer layer of the lime (see "How to Zest Citrus," page 30), and set it aside. Cut the lime in half (ask an adult for help, if needed). Squeeze the juice from both halves into another small bowl and pour the juice into the blender.

4. **blend + pour + sprinkle** Put the lid on the blender and blend until smooth. Pour the smoothie into glasses, and sprinkle with the lime zest. Pure magic!

TIP

Feel free to swap out the
instant oatmeal for cereal.
Puffed rice cereal would be
otherworldly, too.

Birthday Cake Surprise

BERRY CAKE SMOOTHIE: FREEZER FRIENDLY · GLUTEN-FREE · NUT-FREE

CHOCOLATE CAKE SMOOTHIE: FREEZER FRIENDLY · GLUTEN-FREE · NUT-FREE

CHOCOLATE CHIP COCONUT SMOOTHIE: GLUTEN-FREE · NUT-FREE

PREP TIME
15 MINUTES

YIELD
1 OR 2 SERVINGS

Welcome to the choose-your-own-adventure smoothie! Make birthday smoothies for yourself, friends, siblings, your favorite grown-up—anyone! Let the birthday person pick their favorite. In the mood for something fruity? Chocolatey? Coconutty? When it's your birthday smoothie, *you* get to choose! Happy birthday!

WHAT YOU'LL NEED

FOR THE BASE:

1 frozen banana, sliced

½ cup milk

½ cup cottage cheese

½ teaspoon vanilla extract

FOR THE BERRY CAKE SMOOTHIE:

1 cup frozen strawberries

2 tablespoons strawberry jam

FOR THE CHOCOLATE CAKE SMOOTHIE:

Warm water

¼ cup dried prunes or dates (without pits)

2 tablespoons unsweetened cocoa powder

FOR THE CHOCOLATE CHIP COCONUT SMOOTHIE:

½ cup canned coconut cream

½ cup ice cubes

3 tablespoons dark chocolate chips

FOR THE TOPPINGS (OPTIONAL):

Homemade Whipped Cream (see page 76)

Sprinkles

TIPS: If you're avoiding sugar, swap out the chocolate chips for carob chips or cacao nibs. Although cottage cheese works best texture-wise, you can also try this smoothie with Greek yogurt instead.

Birthday Cake Surprise, *continued*

● ●

1. **choose** Choose the smoothie you are going to make: Berry Cake, Chocolate Cake, or Chocolate Chip Coconut.

2. **thaw** Start the base: Take the banana out of the freezer and let it thaw on the counter for 5 minutes.

3. **add** Add the milk to your blender. Add the banana, cottage cheese, and vanilla.

4. **blend + proceed** Put the lid on the blender and blend until smooth. Then, proceed to add your flavor!

   FOR THE BERRY CAKE SMOOTHIE: Add the strawberries and strawberry jam to the blender with the base ingredients. Put the lid on the blender and blend again until smooth.

   FOR THE CHOCOLATE CAKE SMOOTHIE: Fill a small bowl with warm tap water, add the prunes (or dates), and let soak for 10 minutes to soften them. Drain the water and put the prunes and cocoa powder in the blender with the base ingredients. Put the lid on the blender and blend again until smooth.

   FOR THE CHOCOLATE CHIP COCONUT SMOOTHIE: Add the coconut cream, ice, and chocolate chips to the blender with the base ingredients. Put the lid on the blender and blend again until smooth.

5. **pour + top + sprinkle** Pour the smoothie into glasses, and top with whipped cream and sprinkles, if you wish. Happy birthday!

Why do we put candles on top of a birthday cake? Because it's too hard to put them on the bottom!

Pirate Smoothie

DAIRY-FREE (DEPENDING ON MILK USED) · GLUTEN-FREE · NUT-FREE (DEPENDING ON MILK USED)

PREP TIME
15 MINUTES

YIELD
1 OR 2 SERVINGS

WHAT YOU'LL NEED

1 frozen banana

1 cup milk of choice

1 tablespoon honey
+ more to taste

1 lime (for zesting
+ juicing)

½ fresh zucchini, peeled

¼ to ½ cup pitted cherries,
peaches,
and/or berries
(fresh or frozen)

TIP To get a lot of juice from a lime, try putting it in hot tap water for 15 minutes before cutting and squeezing it. You'll get nearly twice as much juice from the lime!

Ahoy, mateys—listen up! Did ye know that, a long time ago, pirates and sailors used to get a terrible disease called scurvy? It happened when they didn't get enough vitamin C in their diet. But avast, mateys! When they discovered that limes be packed with vitamin C, they brought them on their long voyages to keep their health seaworthy!

1. **thaw + pour** Take the banana out of the freezer and let it thaw on the counter for 5 minutes. Pour the milk and honey into the blender.

2. **zest + cut + squeeze + add** Use a grater or zester to scrape off the green outer layer of the lime (see "How to Zest Citrus," page 30), not the bitter white part, and add it to the blender. Cut the lime in half (ask an adult for help, if needed). Squeeze the juice from one of the lime halves into a small bowl and pour the juice into the blender. Add the banana.

3. **chop + add + blend** Chop the zucchini into small pieces (ask an adult for help, if needed) and add them to your blender. Add the cherries. Put the lid on the blender and blend until smooth and thick.

4. **taste + blend + pour** Taste the smoothie. Does it taste sour? If so, add some honey. Put the lid on the blender, blend it again, then pour the smoothie into glasses. Cheers, mateys, and down the hatch!

Peace, Love + Granola

DAIRY-FREE (DEPENDING ON MILK USED) · GLUTEN-FREE

PREP TIME
20 MINUTES

YIELD
1 OR 2 SERVINGS

WHAT YOU'LL NEED

Warm water

5 dried apricots

½ cup milk

⅓ cup granola

½ teaspoon almond extract

1 cup frozen peaches

1 lemon (for squeezing or zesting)

Have you heard of the hippie movement of the 1960s? Hippies wore tie-dyed T-shirts and supported peace, love, the earth, and healthy foods like granola. Today, granola isn't just for hippies. Everyone loves granola, and it's totally far-out in smoothies!

1. **soak + drain** Fill a small bowl with warm tap water, add the apricots, and let soak for 10 minutes to soften them. Drain the water.

2. **fling + add** Fling the apricots, milk, granola, and almond extract into your blender. Add the peaches.

3. **cut + squeeze + zest** Cut the lemon in half (ask an adult for help, if needed). Squeeze the juice from both halves into a small bowl, remove any seeds, and pour the juice into the blender. If you prefer, leave the fruit whole, zest it (see "How to Zest Citrus," page 30), and add a pinch of zest instead.

4. **blend + pour** Put the lid on the blender and blend until smooth. Pour the smoothie into glasses. Enjoy, and peace out!

TIP Apricots are one of the easiest fruits for making jam. They contain pectin, a natural thickener. Recipes for jam often include pectin as an ingredient, but apricots already have pectin in them, so you don't have to add it! Try making some apricot jam to drizzle over your smoothies!

What did the milk say to the granola? We're cereal-sly great together!

Sweet Summer Watermelon Refresher

5 INGREDIENT · DAIRY-FREE · FREEZER FRIENDLY · GLUTEN-FREE · NUT-FREE

PREP TIME
15 MINUTES

YIELD
1 OR 2 SERVINGS

WHAT YOU'LL NEED

2 cups seedless watermelon chunks

2 teaspoons pure maple syrup

5 to 10 fresh mint leaves

1 lime (for juicing)

1 cup water

Watermelons are mostly made of water, which can explain why they're so refreshing to eat on a hot day. They keep you hydrated and are filled with nutrients. And here's a fun fact: The heaviest watermelon ever recorded weighed over 350 pounds—about as heavy as a fully grown panda!

1. **add** Add the watermelon, maple syrup, and mint leaves to your blender.

2. **squeeze + pour** Cut the lime in half (ask an adult for help, if needed). Squeeze the juice from both halves into a small bowl, and pour the juice into the blender. Add the water.

3. **blend + pour** Put the lid on the blender and blend until smooth. Pour the smoothie into glasses, and give a toast to a drink that's truly *one in a melon*!

TIP Some people like to roast watermelon seeds, toss them in salt, and then enjoy them as a snack, like pumpkin seeds—try it sometime!

Why did the cantaloupe jump into the water? Because it wanted to be a watermelon!

Cheerful Chia Pineapple Blast-Off!

GLUTEN-FREE

PREP TIME
15 MINUTES

YIELD
1 OR 2 SERVINGS

WHAT YOU'LL NEED

¾ cup plain yogurt

½ teaspoon chia seeds

1 small handful of fresh basil leaves (about 6 large leaves)

1 teaspoon honey

1 heaping tablespoon nut or seed butter

¼ cup frozen pineapple chunks

Chia seeds are small, round seeds that, when wet, expand and become gel-like. In fact, they can hold twelve times their weight in liquid! These tiny seeds are great for smoothies because they're loaded with nutrients and fiber, which keeps you full. You won't taste them much—the pineapple and basil are the flavor stars here.

1. **add + blend** Add the yogurt to your blender. Add the chia seeds, then add the basil leaves. Put the lid on the blender, and blend for 1 full minute.

2. **add** Add the honey, nut butter, and pineapple.

3. **blend + pour** Put the lid back on the blender and blend until smooth. Pour the smoothie into glasses and *"chia-eers!"*

TIP Spread chia seeds soaked in water on a damp sponge, mist it regularly with water, and watch the seeds sprout and grow into tiny plants! They're safe to eat if you use a new, clean sponge. Use the sprouts in sandwiches or salads—or better yet, smoothies!

How do you know if the smoothie you're drinking is making you happy? You feel chia-ful!

Nutty Blueberry Bonanza Blend

GLUTEN-FREE

PREP TIME
15 MINUTES

YIELD
1 OR 2 SERVINGS

WHAT YOU'LL NEED

½ lime (for juicing)

1 cup buttermilk (see Tip)

2 heaping teaspoons honey

1 tablespoon almond butter or silken tofu

1 cup fresh or frozen blueberries

1 cup frozen mango chunks

Want to know what makes this smoothie taste so good? The sweet and juicy mango, tart blueberries, tangy buttermilk, and nutty almonds each bring their own unique flavor to the team, and together they make an irresistible blend! Speaking of almonds—they aren't actually nuts—they're seeds from the fruit of the almond tree. How delicious is that?

1. **squeeze + pour + add** Squeeze the juice from the lime half into a small bowl. Pour the lime juice and buttermilk into your blender. Add the honey, almond butter, blueberries, and mango.

2. **blend + pour** Put the lid on the blender and blend until smooth. If the almond butter sticks to the sides, turn off the blender, unplug it, uncover it, and use a rubber spatula to scrape down the sides. Cover and blend again. Pour the smoothie into glasses, take a sip, and say, "Almond joying this!"

TIP For a nondairy smoothie, swap the buttermilk for 1 cup almond milk or rice milk with a squeeze of lemon juice.

What is blue and goes up and down? A blueberry in an elevator!

Mango Lassi

5 INGREDIENT · GLUTEN-FREE · NUT-FREE

PREP TIME
15 MINUTES

YIELD
1 OR 2 SERVINGS

WHAT YOU'LL NEED

1 cup plain yogurt

1 tablespoon honey

½ cup frozen mango chunks

1 pinch of ground cardamom (see Tip)

Lassis often include spices like cumin or salt, but this delicious mango lassi uses cardamom, known as the "queen of spices." Cardamom has been used in India for thousands of years—it's added to many dishes and is considered a symbol of prosperity and good luck.

1. **add** Add the yogurt and honey to your blender. Add the mango and cardamom.

2. **blend + pour** Put the lid on the blender and blend until smooth. Pour the smoothie into glasses, and *mmmmmmarvel* at how good it tastes!

TIP Don't have cardamom? That's okay—use cinnamon instead.

How do you make a mango shake? Give it a scare!

Getting Figgy Smoothie

FREEZER FRIENDLY · GLUTEN-FREE

PREP TIME
15 MINUTES

YIELD
1 OR 2 SERVINGS

WHAT YOU'LL NEED

½ cup milk

½ cup plain yogurt

1 banana

2 fresh figs, stems removed

1 tablespoon nut or seed butter

1 teaspoon honey

Figs are great for your digestive health. And fun fact? According to Guinness World Records, the oldest tree known to be planted by a human is a fig tree that's 2,300 years old! In this smoothie, figs come together with banana and nut butter to make the perfect FIG-me-up breakfast!

1. **add + peel + add + blend** Add the milk and yogurt to your blender. Peel the banana and add it to the blender. Add the figs. Put the lid on the blender and blend until smooth.

2. **add + blend** Add the nut butter and honey to the blender. Put the lid back on the blender and blend some more.

3. **pour + enjoy** Pour the smoothie into glasses, and enjoy the fig-tastic taste!

TIP Soft, sweet, juicy figs come in a variety of colors like green, purple, and brown. The good news is that all of them work in this recipe! (Go FIG-ure!)

What did the chef say when she spilled her smoothie? No fig deal!

Plummy Yummy

GLUTEN-FREE · NUT-FREE

PREP TIME
15 MINUTES

YIELD
1 OR 2 SERVINGS

WHAT YOU'LL NEED

½ cup cranberry juice (or cooled hibiscus tea)

¼ cup full-fat coconut milk

¼ cup plain yogurt

¼ teaspoon vanilla extract

2 large fresh plums

2 teaspoons honey

½ cup frozen seedless red grapes

Why did the grape stop in the middle of the road?

Because it ran out of juice!

And why did the plum run after the grape?

Because they were raisin' a fuss!

● ● ● ● ● ● ● ● ● ● ● ● ● ● ●

1. **add** Add the juice to your blender. Add the coconut milk, yogurt, and vanilla.

2. **cut + toss + add** Cut open the plums (ask an adult for help, if needed) and remove the pits. Toss the plums into the blender. Add the honey and frozen grapes.

3. **blend + pour** Put the lid on the blender and blend until smooth. Pour the smoothie into glasses for PLUMTASTIC perfection!

TIP For a fun way to serve this smoothie, add some grape kabob garnishes. Grab some toothpicks or small wooden skewers and carefully slide some washed grapes, one by one, onto the toothpicks. Mix and match different-colored grapes for a festive visual effect!

Why did the plum cross the road? *To prove it wasn't a "chicken"!*

Smoothie
Bowls

Berry Nice Cream Bowl

5 INGREDIENT · GLUTEN-FREE · NUT-FREE

PREP TIME
25 MINUTES

YIELD
1 OR 2 SERVINGS

WHAT YOU'LL NEED

FOR THE SMOOTHIE:

1 cup frozen berries

½ cup heavy whipping cream

1 teaspoon honey (or agave nectar)

FOR THE TOPPINGS (OPTIONAL):

Dried berries

Chia seeds

Sliced banana

Dried coconut

Cocoa powder

Fresh mint or basil leaves

Before modern refrigerators and electric blenders, people had to hand-crank sweet cream in a metal pail surrounded by ice and salt to make ice cream. Since salt lowers the freezing point of water, the ice didn't melt as quickly, and the sweet cream had more time to freeze. Today, you can whip up this yummy semifrozen smoothie bowl in well under an hour!

1. **add + pour** Add the berries to your blender. Pour in the heavy cream and honey.

2. **blend + scoop + freeze** Put the lid on the blender and blend until smooth. Scoop the smoothie into an airtight container, and pop it into the freezer for at least 10 minutes, or up to 1 hour.

3. **check + spoon** Check on your nice cream. Is it ready to eat yet? The smoothie should be firm but easily scoopable and not fully frozen. Spoon the smoothie into a bowl.

4. **top + enjoy!** Top your smoothie bowl with your toppings of choice. Now, that's a *berry* nice treat!

TIP Want to make the easiest ice cream ever? Toss two peeled frozen bananas into your blender and whip them up until smooth and thick. Enjoy or store your 'nana nice cream in an airtight container in the freezer.

What do you call a sad raspberry? A blueberry.

Saturday Morning Cereal Smoothie Bowl

NUT-FREE (WITHOUT ALMOND TOPPING)

PREP TIME
15 MINUTES

YIELD
1 OR 2 SERVINGS

WHAT YOU'LL NEED

FOR THE SMOOTHIE:

¾ cup milk

½ cup plain or Greek yogurt

2 tablespoons honey

¼ teaspoon vanilla extract

½ cup frozen strawberries

½ cup frozen blueberries

¾ cup healthy, fruity cereal (or puffed rice cereal) + more for sprinkling

FOR THE TOPPINGS (OPTIONAL):

Jam (see Tip)

Pomegranate seeds

Fresh banana slices and/or berries

Honey

Yogurt chips

Are you ready for a *cereal*-ously cool fun fact? The first cold breakfast cereal was a lucky mistake! Nutritionist James Caleb Jackson was trying to invent a baked, crunchy snack food that tasted like graham crackers. But—oops—the pieces came out way too dry and were really hard to eat. He soaked them overnight in milk, and *voilà*, the first cold breakfast cereal was invented by mistake!

1. **lob + blend** Lob the milk and yogurt into your blender. Add the honey and vanilla. Put the lid on the blender and blend for 30 seconds.

2. **add + blend** Add the frozen berries and cereal to the blender. Cover the blender again and blend until creamy and thick.

3. **spoon + top + dive in!** Spoon the smoothie into a bowl and sprinkle with more cereal. Have fun layering the rest of your toppings. Then, dive right in, spoon first!

TIP Make your own jammy drizzle! Put 2 tablespoons of your favorite jam into a small bowl. Whisk the jam to break up any clumps. Stir in a tiny amount of water to thin out the jam, and drizzle it over your smoothie bowl.

Sour Power Key Lime Crush

DAIRY-FREE (WITHOUT WHIPPED CREAM) · FREEZER FRIENDLY · GLUTEN-FREE (WITHOUT GRAHAM CRACKERS)

PREP TIME
25 MINUTES

YIELD
1 OR 2 SERVINGS

WHAT YOU'LL NEED

FOR THE SMOOTHIE:

Warm water

2 soft dates (without pits)

¼ cup unsweetened nut milk

1 tablespoon honey

1 teaspoon vanilla extract

½ cup frozen cauliflower

1 frozen avocado

3 key limes (for zesting + juicing; see Tip)

FOR THE TOPPINGS (FOR MORE IDEAS SEE "YUMMY MIX-INS: CHEF CHALLENGE," PAGE 38):

Whipped cream (optional)

Chopped macadamia nuts or almonds

Crushed graham crackers

Grated lime zest

Wait, cauliflower in a smoothie bowl? It sounds wacky, but it's super delicious! The frozen cauliflower gives a thick and creamy texture and lets the star of the recipe—key lime—take the limelight (get it?).

1. **soak + drain** Fill a small bowl with warm water, add the dates, and let soak for 10 to 15 minutes to soften them. Drain the water.

2. **add** Add the dates, milk, honey, vanilla, cauliflower, and avocado to the blender.

3. **zest + squeeze** Use a grater or zester to scrape off the green outer layer of 1 key lime (see "How to Zest Citrus," page 30) into a small bowl, and set it aside for topping. Zest the other 2 key limes into a separate bowl. Cut all the limes in half (ask an adult for help, if needed). Squeeze the juice from the lime halves into the second bowl, and pour the juice and zest into the blender.

4. **blend + scoop + sprinkle** Put the lid on the blender and blend until smooth. Scoop the smoothie into a bowl and top with whipped cream, if desired. Sprinkle the nuts and crackers around the edges of the bowl to look like a piecrust. Top with the lime zest.

TIP Key limes are smaller, rounder, and sweeter than regular limes. You can use regular limes, also known as Persian limes, instead. Although frozen cauliflower is best for the creaminess and texture, you can substitute half a frozen banana for the cauliflower in this recipe.

Rockin' Raspberry Smoothie Bowl

GLUTEN-FREE · NUT-FREE

PREP TIME
15 MINUTES

YIELD
1 OR 2 SERVINGS

WHAT YOU'LL NEED

FOR THE SMOOTHIE:

1 frozen banana

¾ cup frozen raspberries

1 cup milk

FOR THE DOLLOP:

½ cup Greek yogurt

1 tablespoon vanilla extract

1 tablespoon honey

Pinch of grated lemon zest

FOR THE TOPPINGS (OPTIONAL; FOR MORE IDEAS SEE "YUMMY MIX-INS: CHEF CHALLENGE," PAGE 38):

Granola

Fresh raspberries

Sliced banana

Sliced pink dragon fruit

Dark chocolate chips

All right, rock stars—get ready to put on a smoothie bowl show in your kitchen! Raspberries, bananas, and yogurt are the perfect band of flavors, creating a rockin' base for your smoothie bowl. And then, all kinds of toppings add some jammin' texture and flair!

1. **thaw + add** Take the banana out of the freezer and let it thaw on the counter for 5 minutes. Meanwhile, add the raspberries and milk to your blender. Add the banana.

2. **cover + blend + spoon** Put the lid on the blender and blend until smooth. Spoon the smoothie into a bowl.

3. **mix + plop** In a small bowl, stir together the yogurt, vanilla, honey, and lemon zest. Plop tiny dollops of the yogurt mixture on top of your smoothie bowl.

4. **swirl + top + rock out!** Decorate your smoothie. Drag a fork across the top to make a pattern, or make swirling circles or stripes. Add your toppings of choice. Rock out with your taste buds!

TIP Don't have a certain ingredient? Don't worry! Smoothie bowls are like art, so get creative and do whatever works for you! Think of different colors, flavors, and textures—especially for toppings. How creative can *you* get?

Love You a ChocoLOT Peanut Butter Bowl

FREEZER FRIENDLY · GLUTEN-FREE

PREP TIME
15 MINUTES

YIELD
1 OR 2 SERVINGS

WHAT YOU'LL NEED

FOR THE SMOOTHIE:

2 frozen bananas

2 tablespoons peanut butter

2 tablespoons unsweetened cocoa powder

½ cup milk

1 tablespoon honey

FOR THE TOPPINGS (OPTIONAL; FOR MORE IDEAS SEE "YUMMY MIX-INS: CHEF CHALLENGE," PAGE 38):

Sliced bananas

Granola

Dark chocolate chips

Chopped salted peanuts

Greek yogurt

My Dearest Peanut Butter,

Your salty, creamy buttery-ness makes my heart melt. Together, we are the perfect couple. A true match made in kitchen heaven, and I cannot imagine being in a smoothie bowl without you!

All my love,

Chocolate

1. **thaw** Take the bananas out of the freezer and let them thaw on the counter for 5 minutes.

2. **add + pour** Add the bananas, peanut butter, and cocoa powder to the blender. Pour in the milk and honey.

3. **cover + blend + scrape** Put the lid on the blender and blend. Is the peanut butter sticking to the sides? Turn off the blender, unplug it, uncover it, and use a rubber spatula to scrape down the sides. Cover the blender and blend again.

4. **spoon + top** Spoon the smoothie into a bowl. Top and decorate with your toppings of choice.

> **TIP** If you don't have chocolate chips or carob chips, you can grate a chocolate bar into flakes, or add almost anything covered in chocolate, like pretzels, raisins, or almonds!

What did the peanut butter say to the jelly? "You're my 'jam'!"

Smoothie Pops

Creamy Coconut Paletas

FREEZER FRIENDLY · GLUTEN-FREE · NUT-FREE

PREP TIME
4 HOURS

YIELD
6 TO 8 SMOOTHIE POPS

WHAT YOU'LL NEED

1 (13-ounce) can full-fat coconut milk

¾ cup cream of coconut

1 cup heavy whipping cream

½ teaspoon vanilla extract

⅓ cup sweetened shredded coconut flakes

Pinch of salt

ice pop molds

On hot summer evenings, Mexican and American families delight in hearing the ring-ring-ring of the *paleta (puh-LEH-tuh)* cart as it makes its way down their block. Paletas are Mexican pops with a cream or fruit base. Fruit paletas are made from fresh hand-smashed summer fruits with juices or herbs.

● ● ● ● ● ● ● ● ● ● ● ● ● ● ●

1. **open + dump + add** Carefully open the cans of coconut milk and cream of coconut. Dump them into your blender. Add the heavy cream, vanilla, and shredded coconut. Add the salt.

2. **blend + pour + slide** Put the lid on the blender and blend until smooth. Gently pour the mixture into the ice pop molds, leaving a little room at the top (because ice pops expand when frozen!). Slide a Popsicle stick into the center of each mold.

3. **freeze + enjoy** Freeze the smoothie pops until completely frozen, at least 4 to 6 hours. Pop the paletas out of their molds, and share them with friends and family. Shout, *"Buen provecho (BWEN proh-VETCH-oh)!"* That's Spanish for "Enjoy your food!"

TIP If you don't have ice pop molds, use paper cups. Just fill the cups with the mixture, cover with plastic or aluminum foil, and poke a wooden Popsicle stick through the covering into the center of the cup. No sticks? That's okay, too—enjoy it with a spoon, like an Italian ice!

Why did the Popsicle go to the doctor? Because it had a "chill"!

3-Ingredient Fudge Pops

5 INGREDIENT · GLUTEN-FREE

PREP TIME
4 HOURS

YIELD
6 TO 8 SMOOTHIE POPS

WHAT YOU'LL NEED

1½ cups chocolate milk

½ cup chocolate hazelnut spread (like Nutella)

1 banana

ice pop molds

Did you know that ice pops were invented by an 11-year-old named Frank Epperson? It's true! On a chilly day in 1905, he left an unfinished cup of soda, with a stir stick still in it, outside overnight. The next day, he found the drink frozen solid, stick and all, and *voilà*—the first ice pop was born!

1. **add + plop + peel + add** Add the chocolate milk to your blender. Plop in the chocolate hazelnut spread. Peel the banana and add it to the blender.

2. **blend + scrape** Put the lid on the blender and blend until smooth. If the hazelnut spread sticks to the sides, turn off the blender, unplug it, uncover it, and use a rubber spatula to scrape down the sides. Cover again and continue blending.

3. **pour + slide + freeze + feast!** Pour the mixture into the ice pop molds, leaving a little room at the top (because ice pops expand when frozen!). Slide a Popsicle stick into the center of each mold. Freeze the Popsicles for 4 to 6 hours or until completely frozen. Feast on the frosty, flavorful, and fabulously fudge-filled frozen dessert!

TIP To remove the smoothie pops from the molds, run the molds under warm water for a few seconds until the pops release.

Why did the cow start eating chocolate pops? Because it was udderly in love with the sweet, creamy taste!

Peach Cobbler Pops

FREEZER FRIENDLY · GLUTEN-FREE (WITHOUT GRAHAM CRACKERS) · NUT-FREE

PREP TIME
4 HOURS

YIELD
6 TO 8 SMOOTHIE POPS

WHAT YOU'LL NEED

6 fresh peaches

1½ teaspoons ground cinnamon

2 teaspoons ground nutmeg (optional)

½ teaspoon ground allspice (optional)

½ cup honey

2 tablespoons pure maple syrup

¼ teaspoon vanilla extract

1 cup yogurt

ice pop molds

Graham cracker crumbs, for sprinkling (optional)

Homemade peach cobbler is a classic dessert, but it can also be a lot of work. Try this smoothie pop recipe instead. It tastes like the best parts of a peach cobbler, with cinnamon, nutmeg, and sweet peaches blended together. It even has a crunchy topping, just like a real cobbler!

1. **cut + drop** Cut the peaches into pieces (ask an adult for help, if needed). Remove and discard the pits, and drop the chopped peaches into your blender.

2. **add + blend** Add the cinnamon, nutmeg, and allspice, if using. Add the honey, maple syrup, vanilla, and yogurt. Put the lid on the blender and blend until smooth.

3. **sprinkle + pour + slide** If desired, sprinkle the graham cracker crumbs into the ice pop molds, making sure to get a little into each mold. Slowly pour the smoothie mixture into the molds, leaving a little room at the top (because ice pops expand when frozen!). Slide a Popsicle stick into the center of each mold.

4. **freeze + enjoy** Freeze the smoothie pops for 4 to 6 hours or until completely frozen. Pop the pops out of the mold and enjoy. Easy as pie, right?

TIP Make your smoothie pops taste like pastries! Add ¼ cup of oats or almond flour to a smoothie for a pastry texture, or ½ teaspoon of vanilla extract or a spoonful of jam for fruity pie flavors.

What do we call the time in between eating peach pops? A pit stop.

Fizzy Rainbow Fruit Pops

DAIRY-FREE · GLUTEN-FREE · NUT-FREE

PREP TIME
4 HOURS

YIELD
6 TO 8 SMOOTHIE POPS

WHAT YOU'LL NEED

½ cup fresh blueberries

5 fresh strawberries

2 fresh kiwis, sliced

3 fresh peaches

2 tablespoons pure maple syrup

ice pop molds

1 (32-ounce) bottle ginger ale

TIP Clean bumpy fruits and veggies with the power of fizz! Add them to a container of cold water. Then, add 1 teaspoon of baking soda for every 2 cups of cold water. Watch the water fizzle for 10 to 15 minutes, then rinse the fruit thoroughly.

Enjoy the pop of a firework any time of the year with this combination of colorful fresh fruits! They're so colorful, sweet, and tasty, you'll want to eat them all day long!

1. **pour + remove + cut + add** Pour the blueberries into a large bowl. With an adult's help, if needed, use a knife to remove the green tops from the strawberries. Cut the strawberries into pieces and add them to the bowl.

2. **cut + scoop + slice + add** Cut the kiwis in half and use a small spoon to scoop the fruit out of the skin. Slice the kiwi fruit into pieces and add them to your bowl.

3. **add + mix** Cut the peaches into pieces (ask an adult for help, if needed). Remove and discard the pits, and add the pieces to the bowl. Add the maple syrup. Use a spoon to mix everything up!

4. **pack + pour + slide** Pack the fruit into the molds, squishing the pieces of fruit against the sides of the ice pop mold. Pour the ginger ale into the ice pop molds, leaving a little room at the top (because ice pops expand when frozen!). Slide a Popsicle stick into the center of each mold (you might have to wiggle and smush the fruit a bit; that's fine!).

5. **freeze + kaboom!** Freeze the fruit pops for 4 to 6 hours or until completely frozen. Pop-Fizz-Kaboom!

What did the ice pop say
to the ice cream cone?
"You're the 'cone'-ly
one for me!"

Strawberry Lemonade Stand Pops

5 INGREDIENT · DAIRY-FREE · GLUTEN-FREE · NUT-FREE

PREP TIME
4 HOURS

YIELD
6 TO 8 SMOOTHIE POPS

WHAT YOU'LL NEED

2 pounds fresh strawberries

1 lemon, washed + more to taste

¼ cup honey + more to taste

¾ cup water

ice pop molds

TIP Do you know the cooking term "macerate?" It's a fancy way to say "smash and sprinkle with sugar." Just set your strawberries in a bowl with a little sugar. It'll draw out the water from the fruit and make it soft and sweet!

A tall glass of cold lemonade is the perfect fix to a summer heatwave. Now imagine a frozen version of that with strawberries! If lemon juice sounds a bit sour to you, try coconut milk instead of water. The natural fats in coconut milk balance the tartness of the lemons.

1. **remove + drop** With an adult's help, if needed, use a knife to remove the green tops from the strawberries. Drop the strawberries into your blender.

2. **cut + add** Cut the lemon in half (ask an adult for help, if needed). Cut each lemon half into wedges. Remove as many seeds as you can see (it's okay if some seeds remain). Add the lemon wedges, rinds and all, honey, and water to the blender.

3. **blend + taste + adjust** Put the lid on the blender and blend until smooth. Taste. If you'd like it sweeter, add more honey. If you'd like it more tart, add more lemon. Cover and blend again.

4. **pour + slide** Pour the mixture into the ice pop molds, leaving a little room at the top (because ice pops expand when frozen!). Slide a Popsicle stick into the center of each mold.

5. **freeze + dive in!** Freeze the smoothie pops for 4 to 6 hours or until completely frozen. Dive into that pop and let out a great big whoop-de-doo for summer!

My Smoothie Recipes

Create Your Own Smoothie

IT'S YOUR TURN! You get to pick what kind of milk, frozen fruit, and nut butter to use, then blend it all together for a delicious surprise! You know all about kitchen skills, flavor combinations, and swapping ingredients, and it's time to let your imagination run wild and see what tasty creations you can invent.

_____'s
Your Name

_____
Adjective

_____
Favorite Ingredient in This Recipe

_____
Shake, Blend, Smoothie, or Smoothie Pop

PREP TIME
15 MINUTES

YIELD
1 OR 2 SERVINGS

WHAT YOU'LL NEED

½ cup _____
milk or juice type

½ cup _____
yogurt type

1 teaspoon _____
superfood, like cocoa powder

1 tablespoon _____
protein type, like silken tofu
or nut butter

1 teaspoon _____
sweetener type

1 fresh _____
fruit 1

1 cup frozen _____
fruit 2

1. **add** Add the _____ and
   milk type
   the _____ to your blender.
   yogurt type
   Add the _____.
   superfood
   Add the _____.
   protein type

2. **blend + add** Put the lid on the blender and
   blend until smooth. Uncover the blender and
   add the _____.
   sweetener type
   Then, add the _____
   fruit 1
   and the _____.
   fruit 2

3. **blend + pour** Put the lid on the blender
   and blend again until fully combined.
   Pour the smoothie into glasses, shout
   "_____!"
   exclamation type
   and share _____
   your smoothie title
   with _____!
   name of friend or family member

_____'s
Your Name

_____
Adjective

_____
Favorite Ingredient in This Recipe

_____
Shake, Blend, Smoothie, or Smoothie Pop

PREP TIME
15 MINUTES

YIELD
1 OR 2 SERVINGS

WHAT YOU'LL NEED

½ cup _____
milk or juice type

½ cup _____
yogurt type

1 teaspoon _____
superfood, like cocoa powder

1 tablespoon _____
protein type, like silken tofu
or nut butter

1 teaspoon _____
sweetener type

1 fresh _____
fruit 1

1 cup frozen _____
fruit 2

1. **add** Add the _____ and
   milk type

   the _____ to your blender.
   yogurt type

   Add the _____.
   superfood

   Add the _____.
   protein type

2. **blend + add** Put the lid on the blender and

   blend until smooth. Uncover the blender and

   add the _____.
   sweetener type

   Then, add the _____
   fruit 1

   and the _____.
   fruit 2

3. **blend + pour** Put the lid on the blender

   and blend again until fully combined.

   Pour the smoothie into glasses, shout

   "_____!"
   exclamation type

   and share _____
   your smoothie title

   with _____!
   name of friend or family member

_____'s
Your Name

_____
Adjective

....
Favorite Ingredient in This Recipe

_____
Shake, Blend, Smoothie, or Smoothie Pop

PREP TIME
15 MINUTES

YIELD
1 OR 2 SERVINGS

WHAT YOU'LL NEED

½ cup _____
         milk or juice type

½ cup _____
         yogurt type

1 teaspoon _____
              superfood, like cocoa powder

1 tablespoon _____
                protein type, like silken tofu
                or nut butter

1 teaspoon _____
              sweetener type

1 fresh _____
            fruit 1

1 cup frozen _____
                 fruit 2

1. **add** Add the _____ and
                        milk type
   the _____ to your blender.
          yogurt type
   Add the _____.
              superfood
   Add the _____.
              protein type

2. **blend + add** Put the lid on the blender and
   blend until smooth. Uncover the blender and
   add the _____.
              sweetener type
   Then, add the _____
                      fruit 1
   and the _____.
              fruit 2

3. **blend + pour** Put the lid on the blender
   and blend again until fully combined.
   Pour the smoothie into glasses, shout
   "_____!"
         exclamation type
   and share _____
                your smoothie title
   with _____!
          name of friend or family member

Conversion Charts

The recipes in this cookbook use US standard measures. All the conversions in the charts below are approximate.

WEIGHT EQUIVALENTS

OUNCES	GRAMS
½ ounce	14 g
¾ ounce	21 g
1 ounce	28 g
2 ounces	57 g
3 ounces	85 g
4 ounces	113 g
5 ounces	142 g
6 ounces	170 g
8 ounces	227 g
10 ounces	283 g
12 ounces	340 g
16 ounces (1 pound)	454 g

VOLUME EQUIVALENTS

US	METRIC
⅛ teaspoon	0.5 mL
¼ teaspoon	1 mL
½ teaspoon	2 mL
¾ teaspoon	4 mL
1 teaspoon	5 mL
1 tablespoon	15 mL
¼ cup	60 mL
⅓ cup	80 mL
½ cup	120 mL
⅔ cup	160 mL
¾ cup	180 mL
1 cup	240 mL
2 cups (1 pint)	480 mL

Index

Page numbers in *italics* indicate photographs.